how to look after your
CAT

how to look after your CAT

The essential guide to caring for your pet cat, including what to expect at every age; feeding; exercise; grooming; play and stimulation; and when to see the vet

alan edwards

veterinary consultant
trevor turner

southwater

This edition is published by Southwater

Southwater is an imprint of Anness Publishing Ltd
Hermes House, 88–89 Blackfriars Road, London SE1 8HA
tel. 020 7401 2077; fax 020 7633 9499
www.southwaterbooks.com; info@anness.com

© Anness Publishing Ltd 2006

UK agent: The Manning Partnership Ltd
6 The Old Dairy, Melcombe Road, Bath BA2 3LR
tel. 01225 478444; fax 01225 478440; sales@manning-partnership.co.uk

UK distributor: Grantham Book Services Ltd, Isaac Newton Way
Alma Park Industrial Estate, Grantham, Lincs NG31 9SD
tel. 01476 541080; fax 01476 541061; orders@gbs.tbs-ltd.co.uk

North American agent/distributor: National Book Network
4501 Forbes Boulevard, Suite 200, Lanham, MD 20706
tel. 301 459 3366; fax 301 429 5746; www.nbnbooks.com

Australian agent/distributor: Pan Macmillan Australia
Level 18, St Martins Tower, 31 Market St, Sydney, NSW 2000
tel. 1300 135 113; fax 1300 135 103; customer.service@macmillan.com.au

New Zealand agent/distributor: David Bateman Ltd
30 Tarndale Grove, Off Bush Road, Albany, Auckland
tel. (09) 415 7664; fax (09) 415 8892

A CIP catalogue record for this book is available from the British Library.

Publisher: Joanna Lorenz
Editorial Director: Judith Simons
Editors: Mariano Kälfors and Elizabeth Woodland
Designer: Michael Morey
Cover Designer: Balley Design Associates
Production Controller: Claire Rae

Previously published as part of a larger volume, *Complete Cat Care*.

10 9 8 7 6 5 4 3 2 1

The publishers would like to thank Paddy Cutts for her invaluable help.

The photographer and publishers would like to thank the following for
their assistance with the photography: Paddy Cutts, Alison Hay, S. and
R. Badger, S. Bagley, G. Black, V. Dyer, C. Fry, Wade and Kirby Heames,
H. Hewitt, B. Hollandt, J. and D. Johnson, R. Lowen, B. and L. Riddy,
Pampered Pets, Colin Clark veterinary practice, Burntwood boarding
cattery, Weycolour Ltd.

PICTURE CREDITS
All photography by John Daniels unless otherwise stated.
t=top; b=bottom; l=left; r=right; c=centre
Animals Unlimited: 16 t; 21 t; 26 t; 34 t, bl; 35 br; 36 t; 41 b; 42 b;
46 t; 48 b; 50 c; 54 c, b; 55 tr; 59 c; 61t; 64 t, c; 70 t; 71 br; 75 c; 87 br.
Janet Boswell: 37 br; 40 br; 46 b. **Chanan Photography, C.A.:** 43 c; 85 b.
Gilly Cameron Cooper: 15 t; 24 t; 35 bl; 48 t; 69 c; 71 tr; 83 tl; 94 br.
FLPA: 6; 8 b; 9 t; 13 c; 15 b; 37 bc; 38 bl, br; 40 t; 41 t; 44; 46br; 50 t;
51 b; 70 bl; 72 t; 73 bl; 74 br; 76; 91 t; 94 tl, tr, bl. **Marc Henrie:** 10; 78 c.
Mac on Mac Design: 20 b; 39 t; 40 bl. **Papilio Photographic:** 7 tl, c, br.
Planet Earth: 7 bl; 9 b. **Warren Photographic:** 14t; 18; 19 t, c; 21 b; 30 t,
br; 31 b; 32; 34 cr; 35 t; 37 t, bl; 38 t; 39 b; 46 c; 49 tl, r; 51 t; 53 bl, br;
54 t; 55 br; 56; 58 t, bl, br; 60 b; 64 bl, br; 65 tr, c, b; 69 bl; 71 tl; 73tr; 74 t,
bl; 75 tr, b; 78 t; 80 t, bl, br; 81 t, b; 82 t, b; 85 t; 86 t, bl, br; 87 tr, bl; 91 b.

Contents

INTRODUCING THE DOMESTIC CAT

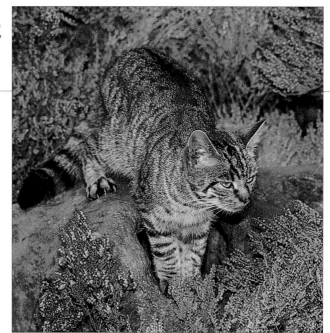

The European wild cat (*left*) was thought to be the ancestor of today's domestic cat because of its tabby markings, but this is now considered unlikely because of its instinctive wariness of people. The more likely contender is the African wild cat (*below*).

Members of the cat family Felidae range from the great, roaring cats such as the lion and tiger to the small domestic cat. They are separated into different genuses (family sub-divisions), not because of their size, but because of differences in their anatomy. These enable members of the genus *Panthera* to roar, while the small cats in genus *Felis* cannot do so. There is a third genus for the cheetahs because they have non-retractable claws. Early in the 1900s there were more than 230 different species of cat in the family as a whole, but now there are fewer than 30. Many became extinct because cats have always been hunted and killed by humans for their fine pelts.

ORIGINS OF DOMESTIC CATS

There is a close relationship between the wild and the domestic cat, but it is uncertain which wild sub-species of the *Felis* (small cats) genus actually made the leap into domesticity. Wild cats are widely distributed and vary considerably in appearance and habits. Northern cats, for example, developed dense, almost woolly coats, while in warmer, southern climes, a fine, body-hugging fur was the norm. Experts ended up with three major contenders for the ancestor of the domestic cat: the European wild cat and its Asian and African equivalents.

For many years, the Europeans believed that it was their wild cat (*Felis sylvestris sylvestris*), which is still found in localized parts of the Scottish Highlands and northern continental Europe. Their assumption was based on the cat's colouring and tabby markings that are common in non-pedigreed cats of today. However, even if the young offspring are reared by humans, they remain very wary, and do not abandon their wild behaviour patterns. This inherent anti-social streak makes them unlikely to have been inclined towards domestication.

On the other hand, the African wild cat (*F. sylvestris libyca*), which still survives in Africa, western Asia and southern Europe, not only has the same number of chromosomes as the domestic cat but is relatively sociable.

CAT ANCESTRY

The wild ancestors of today's domestic cat were among the first carnivores that evolved during the late Eocene and early Oligocene periods of pre-history over 35 million years ago. But it was another family of carnivores, the dogs, Canidae, that became the first animal companions of human beings. Stone Age man took advantage of the dog's superior sensory

powers to help him hunt, and this provided a sound basis for an ongoing relationship. It was not until people graduated into a more settled agricultural way of life that cats became part of the domestic scene.

Small feline skeletons have been found in Stone Age archaeological sites, usually with the remains of other small wild animals such as badgers, which suggests that the cats were killed for their meat or pelts. The first evidence of cats actually living in some tentative relationship with humans was found in a New Stone Age site in Jericho in the Middle East, dating from about 9,000 years ago. However, it is unlikely that domestic cats, living in a relationship with humans similar to that of today, emerged until around 3,500 years ago in ancient Egypt.

CLASS MAMMALIA

ORDER HERBIVORA (Herbivores)   ORDER CARNIVORA (Carnivores)

Family Felidae (Cats)

Panthera (roaring cats) including lion, leopard, tiger, snow leopard, jaguar, clouded leopard

Felis (small cats)

Acinonyx (cat with non-retractable claws)

cheetah

Felis manul Manul[2]

Felis sylvestris libyca (African wild cat[3]) *Felis sylvestris sylvestris* (European wild cat[1]) and many other small cat species

1 May have bred with the early domesticated cats that reached Europe
2 A possible ancestor of longhaired cats
3 The most likely ancestor of most domestic cats

✦ ABOVE LEFT
The leopard is in a different genus from the small cat not because it is bigger, but because the anatomy of its larynx enables it to roar.

✦ RIGHT
Every member, big and small, of the cat family is built to be an efficient killer. The tiger, the largest of the *Panthera* species, is one of the most powerful predators of all.

The lion is another roaring cat of the genus *Panthera*. However, it is quite clearly in the same family as the domestic cat, with its flexible, muscular body, a typically short, rounded head, and large eyes.

The cheetah is in a separate genus because it has non-retractable claws. However, it is closely related to the puma (also known as the mountain lion or cougar), which can retract its claws.

Both this sub-species and the Asian desert cat (*F. sylvestris ornata*) often live on the outskirts of human settlements and are fairly easily tamed. Significantly, remains of the African wild cat have been found in caves lived in by ancient man, and it is generally accepted as the ancestor of most of today's domestic cats. *F. sylvestris libyca* (abbreviated to *F. libyca*) is, in fact, very similar to the Abyssinian breed of today – lithe, long-faced with large ears, and with a ticked, or agouti (dark-tipped) tan coat.

THE PATH TO DOMESTICATION

Our ancestors may simply have hunted and killed these cats, both as a food source and for their pelts. However, as humans were developing an agrarian society based on crops that would have attracted rodents, it is also possible that the kittens were tamed and used to control pests. This would also have been in the cat's interests – keeping the scavenger population under control provided a regular concentration of well-fed prey.

In 1865, Francis Galton, a British scientist who specialized in the study of heredity and intelligence, defined the essential qualities of the early domestic animal. It would need to be useful, easy to tend, able to breed freely, and above all (in the case of the dog and cat, for example), be comfort loving and have a liking for humans. There is also a hypothesis that the process of domestication from wild, savage feline may have been accelerated by genetic mutation. Genes, the building blocks for a living creature, include patterns for behaviour as well as the size and general conformation of the adult. A fault in the genes that control behaviour patterns could, at some time, have created a cat that was

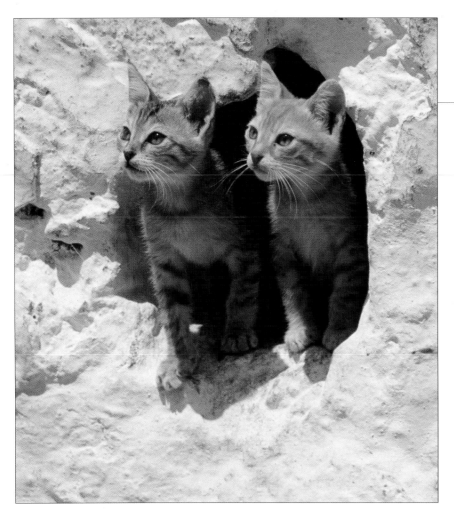

◆ LEFT
Feral cats, like these on a Greek island, tread a
fine line between the wild and the
domesticated; they invariably live – and breed
prolifically – in towns and villages.

coat qualities that resemble those of the modern domesticated cat. It also seems that in such cross-matings, the genetic trait for domestication in one sub-species can strongly affect a more savage temperament in the other. The most recent example of this is the domestic cross with *F. bengalensis bengalensis* (Asian leopard cat) to produce the pedigree variety known as the Bengal. Successive generations enhanced the domesticated qualities of this new breed. (The registration organizations for pedigreed cats in some countries, notably the Cat Fanciers' Association in the United States, do not recognize this breed or any other developed from cross-matings of domestic cats with wild cats, although the Governing Council of the Cat Fancy in the United Kingdom does.)

temperamentally unwilling to leave a juvenile (kittenish) dependency state. This, coupled with a ready supply of food from the human farmers, created an environment in which the mutual advantages of domestication were explored. The kitten-cat gained warmth, comfort and a secure environment in which to breed, and its offspring were valued as an ongoing supply of rodent exterminators. This made the spread of the genetic fault creating the socially valuable domesticated cat inevitable.

The domestication process may well have been accelerated as the African wild cat spread from warm southern and eastern regions and cross-mated with its northern European relation. It has been found recently that cross-matings of these sub-species produce animals with

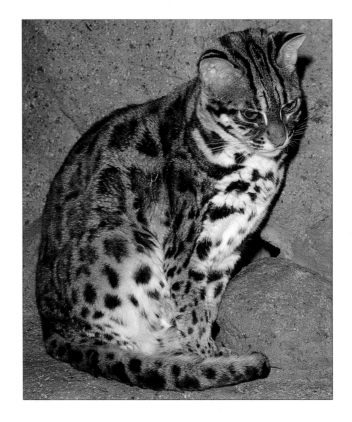

◆ LEFT
The Asian leopard cat (*Felis bengalensis bengalensis*) is a wild species that has been crossed with a domestic cat to produce a new pedigree, the Bengal.

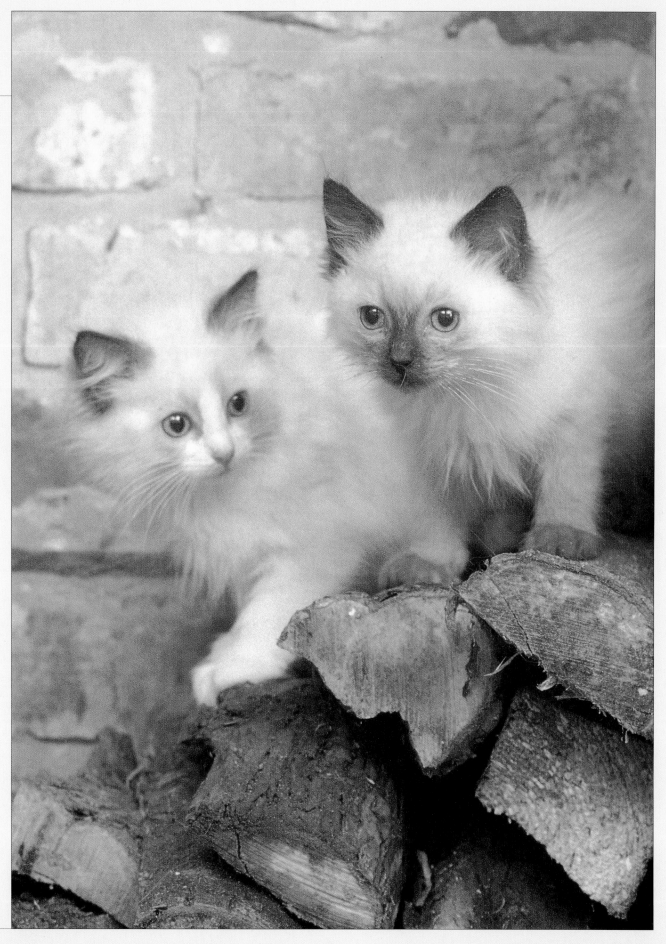

Choosing the Right Cat

Many households are entirely suitable for a cat, or even a companionable pair of cats, but it is important to consider the effects a cat will have on the household. Although they are known for their independence of character, cats do need care and attention. A normal, healthy cat may live for fourteen years or more, and you need to consider whether you can stand such a long-term responsibility and commitment. Cats may all be roughly the same size and shape, but they vary a great deal in temperament, interests and needs. Before you buy a cat, it is wise to look at your lifestyle and home, and consider the type of cat that will happily fit in with it.

◆ FACING PAGE
Ragdoll kittens like these will grow into calm, good-natured adults that enjoy comfort and should adapt happily to an indoor lifestyle.

◆ LEFT
A lively Ocicat may not be of the ideal temperament to be confined to an indoor life.

LONGHAIR OR SHORTHAIR?

Having a longhaired cat requires you to set aside some time every day to groom it, to keep the coat free from tangles and matting. At the other extreme, the almost hairless Sphynx cat needs extra care as it is very susceptible to temperature change and skin problems.

If you are living in a hot, humid climate, a longhaired cat (even if it sheds its cold-weather coat) is not a wise choice unless it is to live in an air-conditioned home. The coat of a Sphynx does not adapt at all to climatic changes, and the cat would need to be kept in a centrally heated environment in cold winters.

If you are allergic to cats, it will probably make no difference whether you have a longhair or a shorthair. Most human allergies to cats are due to the proteins in the scurf (dander) or in the dried saliva covering the hair.

✦ ABOVE
The Maine Coon Cat is a breed with a semi-longhaired coat, which will not need as much extra care as the long fur of a Persian cat.

✦ BELOW
The fur of the Devon Rex cat is fine and wavy and can be so delicate in places that it is broken just by the cat's own grooming. Grooming should be with a very soft bristled brush.

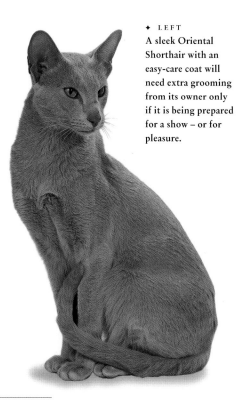

✦ LEFT
A sleek Oriental Shorthair with an easy-care coat will need extra grooming from its owner only if it is being prepared for a show – or for pleasure.

✦ RIGHT
This Persian cat has a splendid long coat that requires a lot of attention. If it lived in a hot climate, however, it would not develop such a full "show" coat.

FUR TYPES

Longhair: soft guardhairs up to 12.5cm (5in) long

Semi-longhair: soft guardhairs varying between 5cm (2in) and 10cm (4in) long

Shorthair: maximum about 5cm (2in) long

Hairless: suede-like coat with no guardhairs

Curly hair: short, soft, often delicate fur with rippled effect

Wirehair: short, bristly coat

BODY TYPES

Cobby: short-legged, stocky body; round, flattish face with small ears, such as the Persian

Muscular: sturdy, medium to compact build; medium length legs and tail; round face, medium ears, such as the American Shorthair

Oriental: long, lithe body; long, slender legs and tail; wedge-shaped face; large, pointed ears, such as the Siamese

GENDER AND AGE

If cats are neutered (altered), there is little difference in behavioural terms between a male and a female. However, a neutered male may be a little more indolent than a female. If you already have a cat in your home, it may be worth going for the opposite sex in your new cat. The established resident is more likely to defend its territory aggressively against a cat of the same sex.

Once sexual urges have been quelled by the neutering process, cats are likely to exhibit their true breed characteristics more strongly. The Siamese cat's attachment to its owner is accentuated, for example, and the Persian becomes even more placid and comfort-loving.

Male cats are generally larger than females. On average, a full-grown, neutered male cat tends to be a little heavier than an entire male, with an average weight of between 5 and 7.5kg (10–15lb). Females are usually about 1kg (2.2lb) lighter. The largest pedigreed variety is the Maine Coon Cat from the north-eastern United States. Male Maine Coons have been

♦ RIGHT
A kitten will adapt to your lifestyle more readily than an older cat, simply because it has not yet fully developed its mature character.

known to reach about 10–12.5kg (20–25lb) in weight. The smallest, or most dainty breed is the Singapura (the "drain cat" of Singapore) at about 2.7kg (6lb), but breeders take care to make certain that their cats fall within the minimum weight range to ensure successful breeding.

♦ ABOVE
Male cats are usually bigger than their female equivalents, although if they have been neutered (altered), they may be a little more indolent.

CHOOSING AN ADULT CAT

It can be easier to give a new home to an older cat than to a kitten. This is especially so if the cat is obtained from a major welfare source which has carried out rigorous health checks. (With a kitten from a private home, the onus of the initial health checks is usually left to you.) An older animal will be more settled in its ways and certainly have an established temperament. A poor temperament due to the cat coming from an environment where it was unhappy, can improve with changed circumstances, but you do not have the fresh start you would have with a kitten. Male cats that have only recently been neutered (altered) may carry some battle scars from their fighting days, but this is a purely aesthetic consideration.

♦ RIGHT
Although the Singapura may have evolved into one of the smallest breeds because of its tough background on the streets of Singapore, it is a sturdy animal.

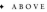

♦ ABOVE
Deciding to take in an adult cat that you have found in a cat sanctuary or home may save the animal from being humanely put to sleep, and it will soon learn to be content in its new, welcoming environment.

WHERE TO FIND A HEALTHY KITTEN

It is essential to choose a healthy kitten. One picked up from the street should be approached with caution.

Despite the pro-neutering campaigns of welfare agencies, unneutered (unaltered) cats do roam freely. This, together with the rapid maturation of the cat, makes it possible for a four-month-old to become pregnant, resulting in the next generation. Such kittens may not be physically strong, they may have been separated from their mother too soon, and are unlikely to have had any veterinary attention or inoculations. Diseases such as feline influenza and feline enteritis can strike a very young kitten and kill rapidly. In addition, feline immunodeficient diseases (feline Aids) may be present.

ACCEPTABLE FREE GIFTS

Some owners allow their cats to have one litter before neutering, and then offer the kittens "free to a good home". They may ask searching questions about your ability to look after the kittens well. Take this in good grace, for these are people who want the best for their kittens.

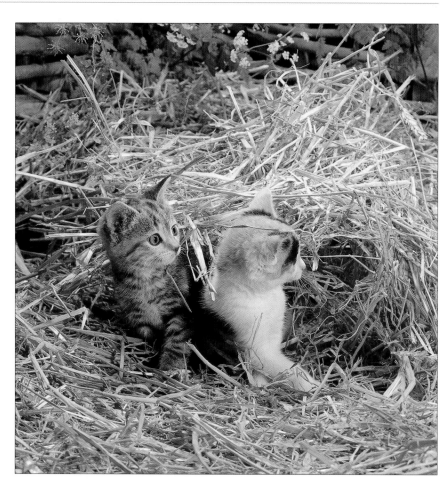

♦ ABOVE
These two farm kittens probably come from a long line of good hunters. Their strength is largely dependent on the physical well-being of their mother and her ability to rear them successfully until weaned.

♦ LEFT
A kitten is hand-fed using a syringe and a special formula milk, as the mother has either died or is unable to take care of her litter.

♦ ABOVE RIGHT
The weight of the hand-reared kitten is checked daily. It needs to gain about 9g (⅓oz) a day, and to be kept constantly warm.

CAT HOMES

If you want to give a home to an unwanted cat or kitten, go to a welfare agency or humane society. There are several big, well-known national organizations as well as many smaller charities that cater for homeless or unwanted cats.

Cats are not usually released to a new owner until they have been given a veterinary check, but the organization may not have had the time or resources for full investigations. This is particularly the case with feline immunodeficiency disease or feline Aids, the test for which is quite expensive. However, coats are routinely checked for parasites and fungal conditions, and the usual vaccinations are often given.

The main welfare organizations usually do investigate thoroughly, including blood-tests to ensure feline

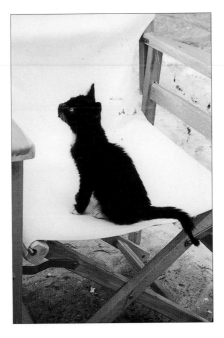

✦ ABOVE
A tiny stray kitten may not be very strong or healthy as it was probably abandoned by its mother too soon – and the mother herself is unlikely to have been in top condition.

Aids and leukaemia are not present. In addition, once an animal has been chosen, they visit the home of the prospective new owner to ensure that it is suitable. Such attention to detail means that they may charge for the kitten, which may make the potential owner think twice before buying. But whatever the cost, it is certainly less than the cost of bringing a stray in dubious condition to peak fitness.

Some pet shops offer kittens for sale only after the necessary veterinary checks and inoculations have been done. However, for the kitten, the stress of leaving its mother, being in the shop, and then being sold on to yet another new environment within a very short time can set them back developmentally. By law in the United Kingdom, kittens must not be sold under six weeks of age. If they appear tiny, it is wise not to purchase.

✦ RIGHT
The last kitten left in a pet shop pen may look appealing, but think carefully before you buy. Will it have picked up parasites from other animals in the shop? Did it have the right medical checks and inoculations before it was put up for sale?

WHERE TO FIND A PEDIGREED CAT

Some breeders advertise in local newspapers. This is a rather hit-and-miss source as there are no guarantees that they are reputable. Some unscrupulous breeders produce kittens of the most popular breeds purely for profit. They may show little concern for either the future welfare of the offspring, or for the breed as a whole.

A far better idea is to ask at your local veterinary surgery or clinic for information on those in the area who specialize in various breeds. Often, if one breeder has no kittens available at the time you want one, he or she will recommend another. Some breeders operate on a large scale and have big catteries, while others are "front parlour" breeders, who may be interested in breeding from just one pet queen. Either can be a good source; the best way to find out about them is by recommendation via a vet

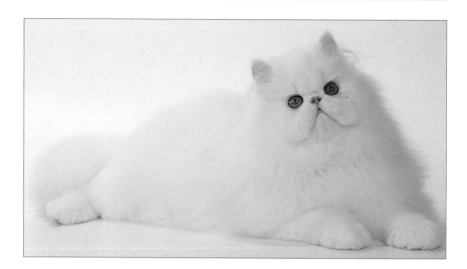

or a local breed club. It is also valuable to visit cat shows well before you actually buy. Here you will find enthusiastic owners and breeders who will explain the advantages and disadvantages of their favourite breeds and let you know of available stock. Find out about cat shows from one of the specialist cat magazines.

◆ ABOVE
The charms of a pedigree cat are displayed by this orange-eyed White Persian. If you want information about where to buy a cat like this, the best place to start is the breed club.

◆ BELOW
The Supreme Show is where you can see the best examples of all the pedigreed breeds in the United Kingdom. There are cat shows in most countries at breed club, local and national levels.

SELECTING A HEALTHY ANIMAL

A kitten from a responsible breeder will have had trips to the vet for inoculations against cat flu, feline infectious enteritis, and possibly chlamydia and feline leukaemia. It will have been wormed and its coat will be free from parasites (such as fleas) and fungal lesions (ringworm).

The queen passes on natural immunity to the diseases to which she is herself immune, through colostrum (first milk) during the kitten's first few days of life. This immunity is effective until the kitten is six to ten weeks of age, when it must be replaced by the artificially acquired immunity provided by inoculations. Before the age of eight or nine weeks, it is best not to interfere with the immunity acquired from the mother.

It is not advisable to take the kitten home before inoculations start if you have other cats. They might be carriers of feline diseases to which the mother of the kitten is not immune and against which, therefore, the kitten has no protection. The certificate from the vet confirming first or complete vaccination carries with it the important implication that the cat is in good health – otherwise the inoculation would not have been administered.

WHAT TO LOOK FOR

The prospective owner can make his or her own immediate checks when selecting a kitten. If you are able to view the entire litter, look for the individuals with evenness of growth and solidity of muscle tone. Male kittens may already be showing a larger skeletal frame than the females. The kittens will be heavy for their size, and their spines should be well-fleshed and not feel ridged and bony.

If you see the litter shortly after feeding, the kittens will probably be sleepy, but if they are inclined to play, you can assess sociability. Frightened, unsociable kittens rush to hide and show fear and displeasure with trembling, bad language or claws – or maybe all three at once! The sociable but sleepy kitten purrs and almost certainly demands that its tummy is tickled. The playful kitten in good health has stamina and a spring in its step. It is alert and may already be displaying intelligence and leadership in play. Rather than you doing the choosing, a particular kitten may well choose you, inviting you to play, and ending up going to sleep on your lap.

The kitten's nose leather should be naturally slightly warm and a little damp. It should not be hot and dry, or have any discoloured discharge from the nostrils. Breathing should be deep and natural with no rasping or snorting. Eyes should be clean and bright with no discharge, tears, staining or redness. The mouth should show nice light-pink gums with no furring to the tongue or ulceration. Ears should be clean and free of wax.

COAT INDICATORS

Clean kitten fur has a lively feel with a warm, naturally wholesome scent, with no evidence of parasites, rough patches or lesions. The most common ectoparasite is the flea, which leaves gritty, granular droppings. Typical sites for these droppings are just above the base of the tail, between the shoulder blades, under the chin and in the armpits. Excessive infestation of fleas may cause a lack of liveliness, and also indicate that the animal may be worm-infested.

Signs of worm infestation are commonly a staring, harsh coat and a bloated abdomen. In severe cases, the kitten may show signs of anaemia and diarrhoea. Check under the tail for staining or signs of soreness, which indicate diarrhoea.

CHECKING AN ADULT CAT

The health check for the older cat is much the same. You need to check that male cats have been neutered (altered). If this has happened recently, they may show some battle scars, but this will only affect their appearance. The most likely place for wear and tear to show is in the mouth. Teeth may be missing or broken, and the gums may show signs of disease, but this can be treated by your vet, who may advise home dental care.

Whatever the age of the kitten or older cat you are thinking of buying, however sweet and charming it is, if you have any doubts about its health, and especially if you have other cats, do not take it home with you.

♦ LEFT
A confident stride, intelligent interest and a perky tail indicate that this 15-week-old Ocicat is a cat of sociable, playful character.

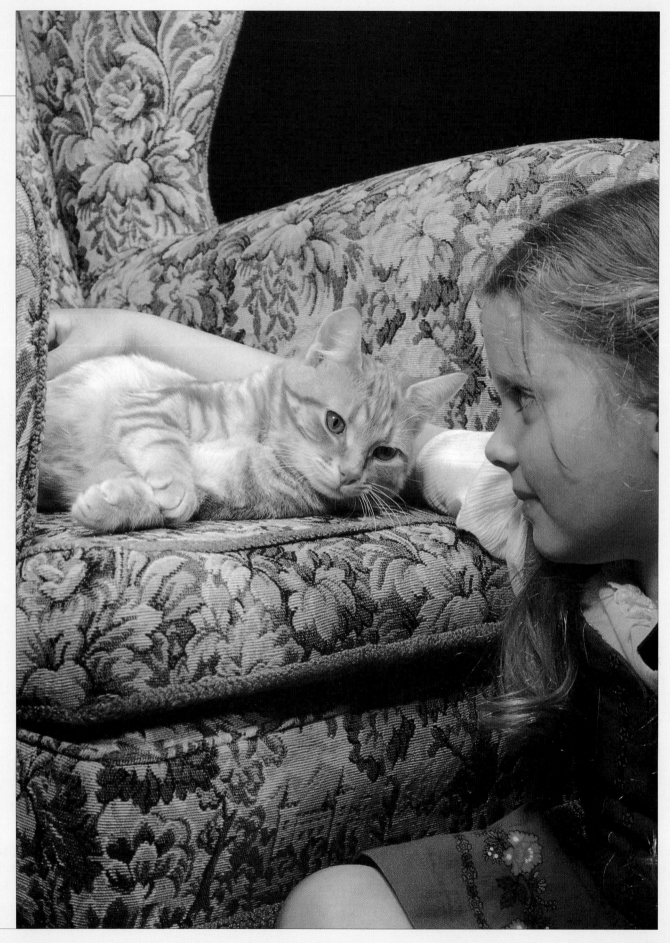

Creating the Right Environment

The domestic life is one in which a pet cat can feel secure in the knowledge of where the next meal is coming from. If you also provide an exciting and stimulating environment in which it can rest comfortably and where there are opportunities to climb and play, your cat will be a well-adjusted and rewarding companion. The financial outlay of buying the right equipment for your cat may seem high, but it is the first step in ensuring it leads a contented life.

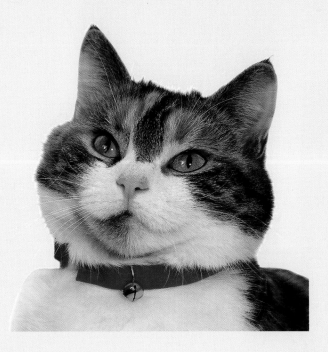

◆ FACING PAGE
Cats may be independent and perfectly able to survive without humans, but as this ginger cat shows, they adapt well to a warm home and loving care.

◆ LEFT
A non-pedigreed cat sports his new flea collar.

SETTLING IN

Acquiring a cat should not be contemplated on a whim but with an awareness of the animal's continuing needs throughout its life in your home. Thoughtful preparation and planning before a new cat arrives is essential if the transition between old home and new is to be stress-free for both you and your pet. A cat needs time and space in which to adjust, and will settle down more easily, too, if all the right equipment is there when it arrives.

FORWARD PLANNING
This will be a new and strange environment for your cat, so before you collect it, check its diet with the breeder or cattery so that you know what it likes to eat and drink and can have some food ready.

 The journey itself may be the first time in a kitten's short life that it has no other feline company. Even an older cat can be disorientated.

While travelling, talk to the animal in a calm voice. Do not be tempted to let it out of its carrier (in a car, for example) unless you have a companion with you who can restrain it.

THE ARRIVAL
A new arrival is a novelty and family and friends will want to be introduced, to stroke and play with the cat, especially if it is a kitten. This exciting time makes particular demands on

✦ TOP
The first sortie in the new home. The cage should be kept to hand so that the kittens can be put back in it until they become used to their new environment, and any other animals in the home can be surveyed from the safety of the pen.

✦ ABOVE
A young ginger cat has settled happily in the cat basket. A favourite blanket brought with it from its first home is an additional comfort.

✦ LEFT
A Siamese half-breed kitten explores the new home. It is important to let kittens explore in their own time, but supervision is advisable in case they become stuck or locked in a cupboard.

EQUIPMENT CHECKLIST

Not all the following are essential; those that are, are in heavy type.

- ✦ **bed and bedding**
- ✦ **litter and litter box**
- ✦ **2 food bowls**
- ✦ **water bowl**
- ✦ **carrier**
- ✦ collar
- ✦ harness and lead
- ✦ identity tag
- ✦ cat flap

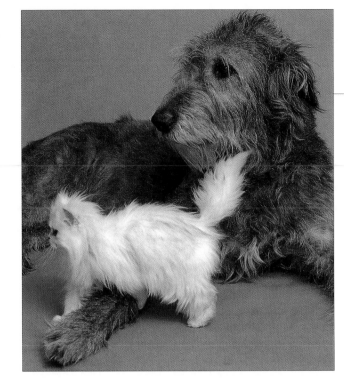

◆ **RIGHT**
Gradual, supervised introductions over the course of a few weeks have enabled this Irish Wolfhound and Chinchilla to feel at ease with each other. However, such close proximity would not be advisable with a pet mouse!

◆ **BELOW RIGHT**
Kittens will quickly seek out the most comfortable places to relax; if you do not want them in your bed, you need to keep the door shut!

When a new cat is tired, it will probably find its bed on its own and it should be left to sleep undisturbed. Cats and kittens sleep more than any other mammal on a daily basis and, for a kitten, adequate sleep maintains and encourages the assimilation of food and enhances correct growth.

If you already have another cat or a dog, confine the new arrival to a small area at first – or even a cage – so that it can get used to where its food, water and litter are in peace, and the animals can adjust to one another in their own time. A cage in the kitchen or living room will provide security for the new arrival and quickly allow it to adjust to any other animals in the household and vice versa.

If you have a baby in the house, it is a good idea to put a cat net over the pram or cot. A cat is unlikely to harm the baby, but could be attracted to a warm, sleeping body and may want to curl up alongside it.

children who, without realizing the implications, may treat the new animal like a toy. However, try to make sure there are not many people around when the new arrival is introduced. It is tempting to rush straight into the living room and let the cat out of the carrier. Instead, take it immediately to where its litter box, sleeping space, food and water bowls are going to be permanently positioned. Such items are part of a familiar routine, which will be comforting. A drink and a little food may be all that is wanted.

EXTENDING TERRITORY
A kitten will want to explore and take in all the new sensory experiences of this new environment. It must be allowed to do this in its own time, and if that means that it wants to scurry about under a kitchen cupboard, out of sight, so be it. Eventually it will emerge and continue its exploration. Allow the kitten to do this at leisure. However, supervision is wise, in case it becomes locked in a cupboard or stuck on a high shelf. Handle the cat calmly and gently. Over-enthusiastic handling

can be very disorientating and may bring out a kitten's defences. Being bitten or scratched does not endear anyone to a new pet, but from the kitten's point of view it was probably justified. By all means stroke the cat as it passes and talk to it. The reassurance of the human voice helps bridge the gap between old and new homes.

HANDLING AND HOLDING YOUR CAT

If you watch a mother cat, you will see how she picks up a tiny kitten by taking hold of the loose skin at the back of the neck and gently lifting. The kitten then demonstrates one of its inborn reflexes, which is to curl up into an apparently lifeless ball. It will not move until its mother puts it down. This loose skin, which becomes far less apparent as the kitten grows, is the scruff or nap. The action of picking up a cat in such a way is called scruffing. While it is possible to lift your cat in this way, scruffing should normally only be considered if absolutely necessary – if instant control is required, for example, when the cat is at the veterinary surgery. For less flexible adult cats especially, it can be an unnerving experience, particularly as they freeze when scruffed.

It is far better to pick up your kitten or cat by placing one hand under the chest, supporting the

◆ LEFT
An established resident cat has become accustomed to a new arrival, and the two now provide extra warmth for each other.

backside with the other hand and then lifting. In this way the animal feels completely secure, with no limbs left dangling. This total support technique is essential if you are holding the cat for any length of time. As you and your cat become more confident, you can try different holds. Avoid tucking

the cat under your arm with its body, back legs and tail dangling like a ragdoll. This leaves most of its weight unsupported and puts a great strain on the internal organs. Many cats do not like being held for too long, and should be gently let down if they start to wriggle.

◆ RIGHT
Avoid surprising the cat when you are about to lift it. When it is relaxed, support the top of the hind legs with one hand and the chest with the other.

◆ FAR RIGHT
When holding or carrying a cat, keep the back end and legs supported. If the cat starts to wriggle, let it down gently; never force it to be held against its will, unless it is necessary.

BEDS AND BEDDING

During the initial settling-in period, a new kitten or cat should be able to settle down within easy reach of both litter box and water. A simple cardboard box placed in a draught-proof spot with an old pillow and blanket is ideal. Then, if there are accidents, or if the cat's bedding becomes parasite-infested, everything can be burnt and little is lost.

Acrylic bedding is widely available, hygienic and easily laundered. Woollen materials, particularly if knitted, are not suitable as claws may become caught. Some cats seem also to be addicted to wool-sucking and chewing and this can cause congestion in the throat or digestive system.

Once the new arrival has settled in, you may want to provide a permanent bed. This can be made of wicker, moulded plastic or padded fabric, but it must be easy to wash and disinfect. Any bedding should be changed regularly. Very soon a collection of cushion beds, old jumpers, carpet-covered houses and other oddities will be adopted. Place these strategically where the cat likes to sleep at different times of the day.

◆ ABOVE
A cat is not fussy about the design of its bed. The advantage of a cardboard box is that if it becomes soiled or worn out, it can be easily replaced.

◆ LEFT
The owner's bed is often a favourite spot, especially if it has comfortable quilts and cushions.

◆ LEFT AND RIGHT
There is now such a range of pet beds available that you can choose one to match your decor. Whether you go for an enclosed, draughtproof and portable model or an open version, the easy-to-wash factor is the most important consideration.

LITTER AND LITTER BOX

♦ LEFT
The most important consideration when buying a litter box is that it should be easy to clean. Use a scoop to remove faeces independently, rather than changing all the litter in the box every time.

A kitten or cat needs access to a litter box if it is not able to go outside when it wants to. The box may become redundant once a kitten is fully immunized and has learnt to use its cat flap into the garden, although it is preferable to encourage your cat to stay in at night. Even when very young, kittens are inherently clean and will not soil their bed. If a cage or crate is being used during the settling-in period, it should be large enough to contain a litter box.

There is a wide range of products available, from basic plastic boxes to covered models with entrance flaps and filters to minimize odour. The key point about litter boxes is that they must be easy to clean, and tough enough to withstand frequent washing and disinfecting. They should also be in a position that is easy to clean. Toxoplasmosis is an infection that can scrape the litter over any faeces deposited, which is does instinctively. Sawdust, woodshavings, cinders, ash and newspapers are not advised; nor are some pine-wood products that can be irritants.

♦ BELOW
The ultimate litter box is not only draughtproof and private for the coy cat, but helps contain odours.

♦ ABOVE, LEFT TO RIGHT
Clay, wood and paper-based litters: some are highly absorbent, others are superfine and form clumps when wet.

be shed in a cat's faeces without the cat showing any signs of disease. It is, however, a hazard to humans, especially pregnant women. Disposal of faeces less than 24 hours after passing and regular cleaning of litter boxes with plenty of water and detergent is effective in the control of toxoplasmosis. Some household products contain ingredients, which, although fine for use in the home, can be toxic to cats. The staff at your vet's should be able to advise on these.

LITTER OPTIONS

The various litter products available should be acceptable to the cat, reduce odour and absorb urine. It should also be easy for the cat to

♦ ABOVE
Kittens are instinctively clean. This feral kitten was abandoned by its mother and when a litter box was provided, automatically began to use it after being shown it once.

FEEDING EQUIPMENT

If you already have perfectly suitable dishes, special purchases may not be necessary. The most practical choices are made of hard plastic, ceramic or stainless steel. All equipment should be easy to clean and disinfect. Discard cracked or chipped ceramic bowls, as germs may be harboured in the cracks. Once any container, new or old, has been allotted to the cat, it should not be used for anything else. Many people feed their cats in the kitchen; if there are dogs around, it is also likely that the cat is fed on a

TOXOPLASMOSIS

Toxoplasmosis affects many animals but cats are the only ones that shed the parasite in their faeces. This only happens for a short time after the cat has become infected and the faeces are only infectious after 24 hours or more. In most cases there are no visible signs of disease or illness in the cat. The infection is carried in the cat's faeces and in 24–48 hours can pass on to humans. Unless their immune system is not functioning properly, humans contracting the infection are unlikely to become ill, but if a pregnant woman is infected, there is a 40 per cent chance that her baby will also be infected. Of these infected babies, 15 per cent may spontaneously abort or acquire some abnormality.

◆ Wear gloves when gardening in an area frequented by cats

◆ Cover children's play areas, such as sand-pits, when not in use

◆ Empty litter boxes on a daily basis and clean regularly with plenty of water and detergent

◆ Use a separate set of feeding equipment for the cat and do not use it for humans; clean regularly

◆ **ABOVE, LEFT TO RIGHT FROM TOP LEFT**
The cutlery for serving the cat should be exclusively for this purpose; plastic lids to cover unfinished tins prevent the food from drying up and the smell from spreading; a simple plastic bowl; a metal bowl; a plastic combined water and food bowl; an automatic feeder.

working surface. In either case it is especially important to maintain strict standards of hygiene to guard against the risk of toxoplasmosis (see box). The feeding area must be easy to clean and disinfect regularly. This is also important for the cat because it has a highly developed sense

of smell and will reject food that has become tainted and hardened. For the same reasons, put down fresh water at least once a day. A closed-off eating area is advisable if you have crawling babies or toddlers.

For the busy owner whose lifestyle makes feeding the cat at regular times uncertain, automatic food bowls with timer switches are available. The cover automatically lifts to reveal food at pre-set times. A water bowl is kept topped up with water from a reservoir, but you do need to remember to change the reservoir frequently.

◆ **RIGHT**
It is more hygienic to put your cat's food on the floor rather than on a working surface where food is prepared for humans.

CARRIERS

It is essential to buy, rather than borrow, a cat carrier. You will need it not only to bring the cat or kitten home, but also for visits to the veterinary surgery – and anywhere else for that matter. Any visit to the vet will quickly reveal that very many owners have great faith in their pets' ability not to escape! They arrive with all sorts of contraptions for carrying their cats; sometimes with nothing at all to restrain an animal which may be in pain, very frightened and invariably highly stressed.

SIZE CONSIDERATIONS

Do not be seduced into buying a sweet, kitten-sized carrier; consider the future and purchase accordingly.

◆ ABOVE
Large cat carriers provide plenty of room for your cat and can double up as pens for the settling-in period. They are, however, awkward to carry.

◆ LEFT
A top-loading wicker basket which could double as the cat's permanent bed.

That cute little fur-ball is going to turn into a considerably larger adult. A carrier of around 30cm x 30cm x 55cm (12in x 12in x 22in) should last into the cat's adulthood. For an extra-large male, it might be wise to go to the next size up. Cats prefer to be in a fairly snug environment if they are experiencing a rare and disturbing event such as travelling, but they do need to be able to turn around and stretch out a little. They also like to be able to see out so that they feel a little less trapped.

If the journey is going to be a long one (over an hour or two), have a carrier that can take a small litter box as well as clip-on water and food bowls. However, if you are likely to have to carry the cat very far, for example, when attending shows, remember the larger the carrier, the more awkward it is to carry. Strained shoulders and backs are not uncommon among exhibitors.

✦ **BELOW**
An easy-to-clean plastic container that might cause loading and unloading difficulties.

✦ **BELOW**
A collapsible cardboard carrier that can be dispensed with after being used to carry an infectious animal.

WHAT IS AVAILABLE

Basic cardboard carriers, preferably coated with plastic, are bought flatpacked, and, when assembled, are suitable for transporting a sick and possibly infectious animal, as they are inexpensive and can be burnt after use. However, they are not suitable for more regular use as they cannot be cleaned and disinfected effectively, and are not durable. Traditionalists choose wickerwork baskets, which come in various shapes, and usually have leather straps and a handle. These are attractive and could double as the cat's permanent sleeping quarters – at least the cat would be less likely to panic if travelling in its own bed.

Openwork wire baskets, especially with the wire covered with white plastic, have veterinary approval because they are so easy to disinfect and the cat is easily visible. The top opening is secured by a separate rod pushed through rigid loops. Moulded plastic carriers with strategically placed ventilation holes are available in a great range of designs, are easy to dismantle for thorough cleaning, and

reassembling is no problem either. Clear moulded plastic (Perspex) carriers with airholes are a less worthwhile investment as the plastic tends to crack and degrade over time. If carried in sunlight, its occupant can quickly overheat.

The most practical designs are those with top access; they are less stressful both for cat and handler.

The cat can be grasped from above and removed without a struggle. With a front-loading carrier, the often frightened animal has to be recovered from the back of a tunnel. It can also be difficult to put the cat back inside.

✦ **BELOW**
If you want your cat carrier to look distinctive or decorative, you could paint it with an appropriate design.

COLLARS, HARNESSES AND LEADS

A collar is not necessarily merely decorative. A tag may be attached to it so that the cat can be identified if it gets lost or injured. An identity tag may be a simple engraved disc or a screw-topped cylinder containing a roll of paper with the cat's name, owner's address and telephone number, and sometimes the vet's emergency number. Magnetic tags that allow your cat exclusive entry to its cat flap can also be fitted on collars.

Most collars come with a bell which rings when the cat moves and will reduce the death toll among garden birds and other potential hunting targets. Some collars are impregnated with an anti-flea substance, but keep a careful check on your cat when you first put one on it, as they can cause an allergic reaction. Signs of irritation around the neck or eyes are the main indications of allergy. A flea collar should never be combined with any other form of flea control.

Collars have two main disadvantages. If worn continuously, as they should be if they are carrying any form of identification, they will damage the fur around the neck,

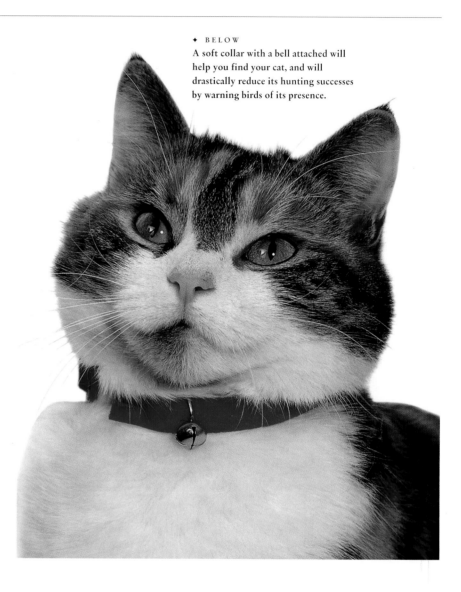

◆ BELOW
A soft collar with a bell attached will help you find your cat, and will drastically reduce its hunting successes by warning birds of its presence.

◆ ABOVE
A soft, padded flea collar with a bell and an elastic section. Flea collars should only be used on cats over six months old. They may cause an allergic reaction in some cats.

◆ ABOVE
A soft leather collar with the all-important elastic section. Any collar you buy should have this, for if the collar is caught the elastic will stretch, allowing the cat to escape unharmed.

◆ ABOVE
Fabric collars, which can be cut to size without fraying, are useful for kittens and small cats. They are cheap enough to be changed regularly, or even to have a selection of different colours.

especially that of longhaired cats. This can be unsightly and is considered unacceptable by many exhibitors; although most show judges realize the reason for any marks around the neck, they may still penalize the cat. Secondly, there is always the fear that the collar can become caught when the cat is hunting in trees or shrubs. However, if it is made of soft leather, suede, or soft fabric and has an elasticated insert, this will stretch if the collar catches, and the cat will be able to free itself. The collar should always be adjusted so that it will slip over the cat's head in an emergency, but not loose enough to allow the front leg to slip through and the collar to lodge under the armpit, which could cause injury.

GOING FOR A WALK

Cat leads are only necessary if you intend to take your cat for walks or if you are taking it to a strange house and need to keep it under control. Some cats actively enjoy this, particularly Siamese. It is not unusual to see this breed travelling on public transport on a lead. However, most cats are naturally resistant to wearing any such controlling apparatus and will fight against it, especially if they become frightened. To take them on a bus or train on a lead rather than in a carrier is foolhardy under any

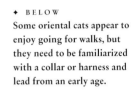

circumstances. If the cat panics, it could either become tangled and hurt itself, or escape. If a lead is worn on a more suitable outing, it should be no more than 1m (3ft) long, and have a fitted harness rather than a collar for attachment. This not only allows more control and comfort, but is more secure. Cats are great escapologists, however, and even the most carefully fitted harness may prove insecure.

Introduce your cat to a harness and lead as early as possible. Put the harness on first by itself, and just for a short time each day. After you have done this for a few days, attach the lead for a short time, several days running, but just leave it trailing. When the cat seems relaxed about the lead, try walking it, first indoors for brief spells, then in the garden, and then in a street where the cat can get used to traffic and people, but do not overdo it!

◆ **LEFT**
Magnetic tags double as a means of identity and a "key" to enable the wearer to go through its cat flap.

◆ **BELOW**
Some oriental cats appear to enjoy going for walks, but they need to be familiarized with a collar or harness and lead from an early age.

◆ **LEFT**
Identity tags can be simple metal discs engraved with the owner's name and telephone number, or an information-packed barrel containing the owner's address and the vet's address and emergency telephone number.

PLAYTIME AND TOYS

Play for a young cat is just as essential for its well-being as it is for a human child. It is particularly important for the owner to play with the cat if it is the only one in the household. Through play, muscles are exercised and conditioned, the brain is kept alert and the eyes bright. And if the owner joins in, it strengthens the bond between the feline and its adopted human family.

At the very least your cat should have a scratching post, which it can be encouraged to use instead of the furniture and soft furnishings. A cat will naturally use surfaces such as the bark of a tree to sharpen and control the length of its claws – they are its main means of defence, and also provide grip when climbing. You can make an indoor scratching post yourself by binding a stout fence post with heavy-duty sisal string or cotton rope, and attaching it to a suitable base. A strip of old carpet is an alternative, but this is not as effective for the cat, as it frays quickly, creates a great deal of fluff, and needs to be

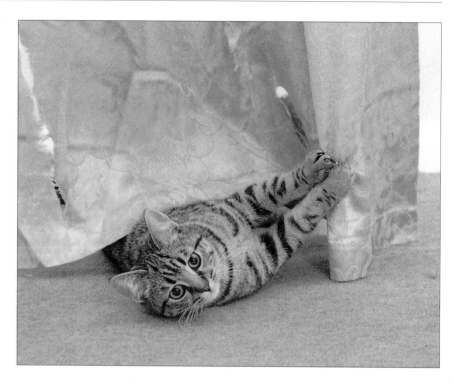

renewed regularly. If you do not mind your cat equipment taking over the home, feline climbing frames of varying size and complexity are readily available. Some are over 2m (6ft) high, with circular supports covered in sisal rope, carpet-covered perches, houses and barrels. They are likely to be found at cat shows, or through advertisements in specialist cat magazines and larger pet stores.

PLAY WITH A PURPOSE

A cat's play is orientated to the hunting process. When a cat swoops after a leaf in autumn, that leaf is an imaginary bird. The ping-pong ball just visible behind a chair leg is a mouse to be stalked, pounced upon and batted around. The screwed-up paper hurled into the air, caught and thrown away to be chased and sent flying again, is being hunted.

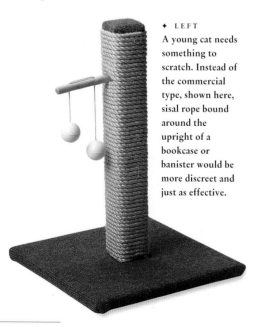

◆ LEFT
A young cat needs something to scratch. Instead of the commercial type, shown here, sisal rope bound around the upright of a bookcase or banister would be more discreet and just as effective.

◆ ABOVE
Being ten months old does not mean that this youngster has grown out of shredding curtains for fun.

◆ BELOW
Kittens enjoy playing with someone, especially if they are an only cat; they will soon become bored playing on their own with a ball.

◆ LEFT
The perfect combination for a family cat –
company, care, attention, and a game that seems
to be tailor-made for cats. Be careful of any
electrical connections, though.

Even in an apparently sterile
environment, a cat will find a scrap of
paper, a lost button, or a shadow to
play with. However, do be careful of
everyday household objects like the
odd button or needle and thread.
Swallowed thread can do even more
damage than a needle as it cheesewires
its way through the bowel.

Do check that any cat toys you buy
are reasonably solid. Some cheap
imported toys may have small plastic
bits that could fall off and be
swallowed. Some plastic materials that
are safe for children can be toxic to
cats. All that is needed can be found in
the home: paper scrunched into a ball
and thrown by the owner for retrieval
up and down the stairs; a paper
"butterfly" tied to a piece of string
and dragged around for the cat to
chase, or suspended from the back of
a chair to bat. Some cats are
particularly fond of hide-and-seek.
For group play, nothing is better than
the great game of the ping-pong ball
rolled around the carpet between
family members and friends, and
pursued by your cat.

◆ BELOW
A clockwork mouse is a poor
substitute for the real thing, as
it has to be wound up, but it is
less messy for
the owner.

◆ RIGHT
You will probably need a continuing
supply of replacement balls as they are
constantly being batted out of sight.

◆ ABOVE
Cats are nature's most efficient predators: a
fabric mouse filled with delectable catnip may
not last long in the grip of this young Ocicat.

◆ RIGHT
Here's a soft, friendly chap to dig your claws
into. Let's hope the bear's eyes are well secured
so that the kitten does not swallow them.

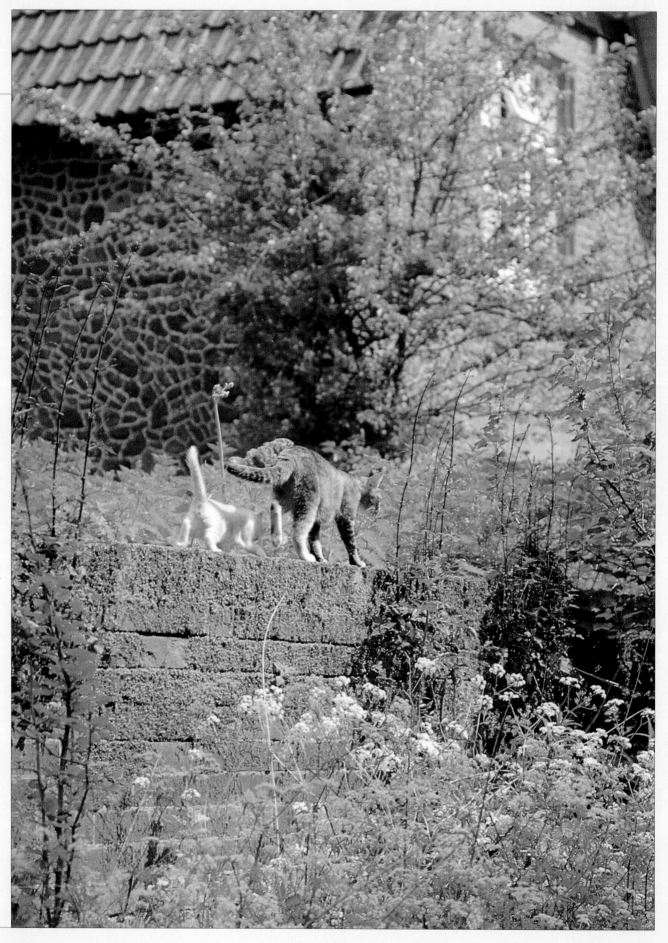

Care at Home and Away

A cat instinctively knows its physical limits; it can also, through learned behaviour and training, avoid potentially dangerous situations. The wise owner strikes a balance between giving the cat the freedom it needs, being aware of the dangers it could face, and protecting it from them.

◆ FACING PAGE
A mother introduces one of her kittens to the outside world. She will teach it survival and hunting skills.

◆ ABOVE
A well-cared-for ginger and white non-pedigree is completely relaxed at home and away.

CONTROLLING A CAT'S TERRITORY

If you live in an apartment block or in a busy urban environment, or your cat is frail or a valuable pedigree, it is perfectly feasible – and acceptable to most cats – to keep it indoors all the time. In some parts of the United States, vets actively recommend this for cats in urban environments.

Because of the balanced pet foods now available, modern cats do not need to go out to supplement their diet by hunting. Outdoor exercise is also unnecessary, as long as the owner provides toys and plays with the cat.

Although cats are nocturnal by nature, it is really unwise to allow much-loved pets to stay out at night. Train them to stay in from an early age and make sure there is always a clean litter box available. This training also ensures that they are equally happy if kept indoors for long periods.

The outdoor cat's tendency to roam and exposure to the dangers of traffic, fighting and infection from other cats, can be reduced at a snip – that is, by being neutered (altered). The sex-drive of a calling queen or an active

♦ ABOVE
A Burmese is attracted to the outside world. Some cats are freedom-loving and do not like being kept indoors.

♦ RIGHT
A ginger kitten has taken over the best armchair. An indoor cat needs plenty of toys and active input from its owner if it is not to become bored and substitute the upholstery for a tree.

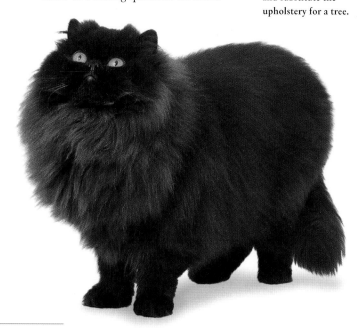

♦ LEFT
A Persian has the comfort-loving temperament suited to an indoor life, and its long coat is easier to care for inside.

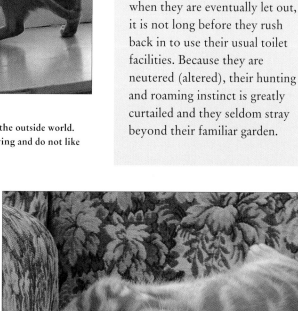

THE MAKING OF AN INDOOR CAT

The consultant, a breeder of Maine Coon Cats, does not let his cats out until they are well over six months old – two to three months after they have been neutered (altered). The cats are trained to litter boxes and so, when they are eventually let out, it is not long before they rush back in to use their usual toilet facilities. Because they are neutered (altered), their hunting and roaming instinct is greatly curtailed and they seldom stray beyond their familiar garden.

tom cat will override any considerations for road safety. The unneutered male cat can hunt over an area of about 11km (7 miles). His desexed counterparts will probably exercise territorial rights over maybe 200m (240 yards) at most.

DANGERS IN THE HOME

There are dangers even for the cat that is kept indoors all the time. Those who live in high-rise buildings should erect netting across open windows and around balconies. The defences can be camouflaged by plants. Even within the house, cats should be allowed access to heights only if they are considered safe. A specific danger area is a staircase with openwork bannisters from which a kitten could launch itself into space – not necessarily landing on its feet. Kittens should be supervised as they explore.

THE ALLURE OF MACHINES

The warmth, the smells and the movement of washing and drying machines attract a cat's attention. Always make sure that the appliance's doors are kept closed when not in use. Before you turn the machine on, check that there is no cat curled inside. The smell of food in a fridge is also enticing. At least if it were to be inadvertently incarcerated, a cat would survive there for some time, as long as there was sufficient air available. It would not, however, survive for long in a freezer. Fifteen minutes would probably be long enough to cause irreversible hypothermia.

PLAYING WITH FIRE

Burns and scalds sustained by cats exploring the source of interesting food smells are not unusual and are sometimes very severe. Cats have been known to dance across the hot rings of an electric cooker, badly damaging their paws.

Electric cables are potential playthings, so make sure no wires are loose or exposed, and if you spot your cat chewing them, conceal the cables beneath a carpet, or cover them with a catproof material such as thick, loose rubber or plastic tubing. A cat will nose around drawers and boxes packed with interesting oddments – but here too, are potential dangers such as pins and paper clips. Tasty, pingy elastic bands may be fun to pick at and chew, but could cause choking and suffocation, and the same goes for lengths of wool or cotton, or plastic film. Cats are also attracted to olives, the stones of which are just the right size to become stuck in a feline throat. Open fireplaces should always be guarded, even when a fire is not lit, for cats like climbing up chimneys and may become stuck or break a limb, or at the very least emerge soot-covered. Electric and gas fires can be equally dangerous. One cat owner was faced with a fire in her living room and some very frightened kittens, after the combined weight of the litter of kittens toppled a highly flammable chair against the bars of a gas fire.

◆ LEFT
A very cosy scene for mother and kitten – however, open fires should always be kept guarded unless you are in the room to keep an eye on your cat.

◆ ABOVE
The washing machine has just been turned off and is still warm, making it a possible spot to curl up in for an undisturbed sleep.

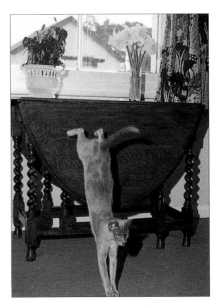

◆ ABOVE
The deliberate leap from the table is well within this cat's capability, but a kitten could hurt itself if it fell or jumped from such a height.

35

ACCESS TO THE OUTSIDE WORLD

It always used to be common practice to put the house cat out at night, so that it could carry out its rodent extermination duties, and to avoid mess in the house. Effective rodent control and the availability of litter boxes have made this unnecessary. Now a cat's freedom is more likely to be dependent upon human work patterns. However, unless you have pedigreed cats which you keep for exhibition and show, or your living space necessitates an indoor lifestyle, you can allow your pet various degrees of access to the outside world.

Some cats automatically confine their territories to the back garden. Others may develop an awareness of the traffic in their area, and avoid rush hours, for example. However, it is difficult to be sure of their abilities, and even quiet streets can be dangerous because of the occasional,

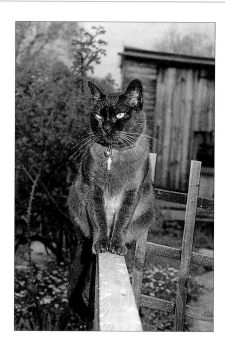

unexpected vehicle. For these reasons, and the risks of territorial fighting and exposure to infection, it is worth exercising some form of control over your cat's freedom to roam.

♦ ABOVE
A Brown Burmese selects a high vantage point from which to survey the surrounding territory.

CAT FLAPS

Cat flaps are cat-sized windows that are fitted about 15cm (6in) from the base of a door. The most practical design is one that is gravity-loaded so that the door automatically closes after entry or exit, and with a clear plastic window so that the cat can look through it before venturing outside.

Flaps are a boon to the indoor/outdoor cat that is not afraid of operating the flap and whose owners are not always home to obey the cat's every whim. They allow both cat and owner a degree of independence from each other. The main disadvantage of cat flaps, particularly when there is no such feline control, is that neighbours or feral cats will soon learn to use them, particularly if delicious food is known to be available on the other side of the flap. This could lead to disease or infection being brought into the home, or territorial fights, or both. One way of overcoming this is to have an electronically operated flap that allows entry only to cats wearing the appropriate collar and gadgetry – usually in the form of a magnetic tag that doubles as an identity tag.

Alternatively, you can allow your cat limited freedom, and, for example, lock the flap at night when you are unable to keep an eye on unwanted visitors. It is useful to buy a flap that can be locked to prevent your cat from going out at certain times, or other cats from coming in. Your cat will soon become used to whatever routine you set.

When you introduce your cat to the cat flap, spend some time encouraging it with your voice and showing it how the door works. Put the cat on one side and call encouragingly from the other.

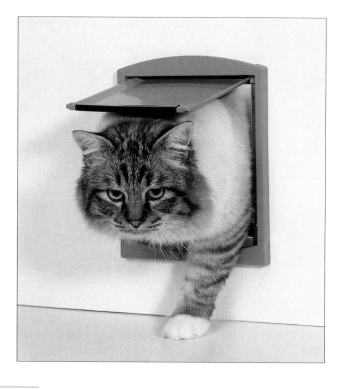

♦ LEFT
A cat will soon learn to use its cat flap with confidence. The flap swings shut when the cat has passed through.

◆ RIGHT
A tom cat prepares for his nocturnal prowl. Many of the small rodents that cats hunt are active as night falls, and this also seems to be a prime time to look for a mate.

After a few tries, it will know exactly what to do by itself. However, it is not unusual for some cats to steadfastly refuse to use a flap – particularly if the flap was introduced after the cat. The same goes for flaps on covered litter boxes.

OUTDOOR CONFINEMENT

Indoor living can be safely supplemented by a secure outdoor area. Areas of a garden can be fenced in with wire or plastic mesh like a fruit cage, or a purpose-built shed or pen can be provided. Climbing plants can be trained to cover the sides to soften the appearance, but take advice on which plants to choose – some are poisonous to cats.

A pen can be constructed in the garden or as an extension to the house (with access via a cat flap). It should be sturdy in structure with wire or plastic mesh stretched between a solid wood frame, and roofed. Features

could include a covered shelter and an outdoor play area with logs, shelves and playthings to keep the cats amused. Such pens are commercially available. In extreme cases, or with very small areas, whole gardens are secured around the perimeter to prevent cats from escaping and, more importantly, other cats from getting in. You can make a framework of stout posts to a height of say 3m (9ft) and attach wire netting between them. If the netting is loosely fitted the cat will not be able to climb up it and there will be no need to roof in the top. The base of the wire should be buried or well secured.

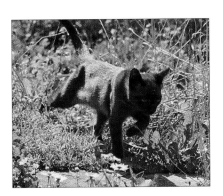

◆ ABOVE
A lithe hunter like this Brown Burmese will be a joy to watch in your garden.

◆ RIGHT
Cats are often attracted to the shelter and warmth offered by parked cars, so always check beneath your car before you drive away.

◆ FAR RIGHT
Cats enjoy fresh air and sunshine from the safety of an outside pen.

IN THE GARDEN

To watch a cat move and play in a garden is a source of delight, but there are dangers. Cats can swim, but are not generally renowned for their ability in this area, and there are cases of accidental drowning each year. The simple solution in the case of a garden pond, stream or swimming pool, is to cover the water with very fine mesh or to erect a barrier to make the area inaccessible to the cat.

Cats do have a wonderful righting ability which enables them to almost invariably land on their feet when falling from a height. However, vets regularly see cats that have been badly injured as a result of falls. If a cat lands on an unyielding surface, it is likely to injure itself if the fall is more than 3–4m (9–12ft), which is equivalent in height to the first storey of a house. The same applies if they fall out of trees. The most common problem with cats climbing is that they become absorbed in either hunting or exploring and end up on a branch too small to turn around on and escape.

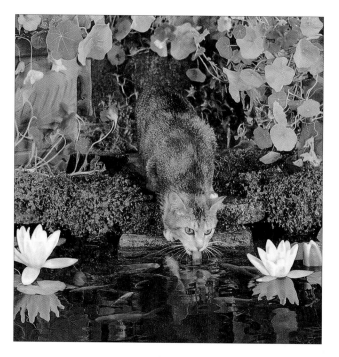

◆ LEFT
Thirst, reflections and goldfish are all good reasons for cats to be interested in water. They are not renowned for their swimming skills, however, and a net over the garden pond is worth considering.

◆ BELOW
Another sticky situation for an exploratory kitten. At this stage of their development, adventurous kittens should be supervised.

This is when the rescue services are called in. Discourage habitual climbers by placing wire netting around the base of favourite or particularly dangerous trees. However, the determined feline may just look for another tree.

◆ LEFT
When maturity and wisdom have taken the place of adventure and curiosity, a garden can be a great place for sunning and relaxation.

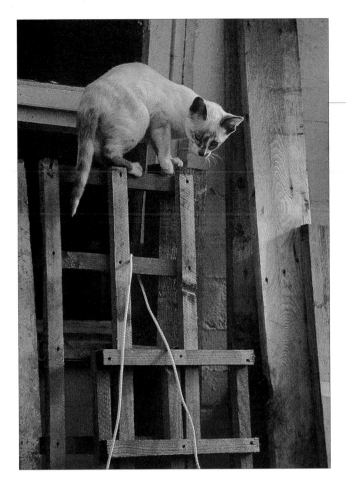

◆ LEFT
This kitten is in
danger. Curiosity
has led it to explore
beyond its limits to a
narrow perch where
its leg could become
stuck, or from which
it could fall.

◆ BELOW
A broken pane of
glass in the garden
shed spells danger
for this cat. If it
attempts an escape
through the hole, it
could cut itself badly.
The lesson for the
owner is to carry out
repairs promptly.

INSURANCE

Compare the cover and terms of
several companies that specialize in
animal insurance before you make
your decision. The owner of a
valuable cat may want to insure
against loss, death or theft, in order
to reclaim the cat's value. More
general policies cushion the owner
against the cost of veterinary bills in
the event of accident or emergency,
injury or disease, but do not cover
initial injections, neutering or
standard booster inoculations. The
annual premium depends upon the
level of cover selected and upon the
insured animal's medical history.
Deciding whether or not to insure
is a matter of balancing what can be
a fairly steep monthly or annual
premium against your ability to pay
any sudden, costly vet's bill. The
alternative, as with any insurance
cover, is to have your own
contingency account to cover
emergency expenses.

Cat breeders sometimes issue
basic health insurance cover notes
with kittens. Cover starts from the
date of sale and is usually valid for
six weeks. After that, the new
owner can continue with the same
policy or seek another one.

TRAPPED

Apart from harbouring dangerous
substances, garden sheds and garages
can become prisons from which there
is no escape. A brief period of captivity
will not do a cat too much harm. A cat
can survive for 10–14 days without
food and almost as long without water,
provided the ambient temperature is
not too high, but the resulting

dehydration and starvation may have
serious consequences for the proper
functioning of kidneys and liver. Such
a physically challenged cat is then prey
to secondary infections it would
normally easily shake off. If you have
not seen your cat for a while, check in
cellars, cupboards, tool sheds and
garages, in case it is trapped. Before
you go away, make sure your cat is
there, and that a neighbour (or the
person looking after the cat) has access
to the house, and any sheds or garages.

◆ BELOW
A farm kitten has found a warm, sunny spot to sit in. Let's hope there are no nasty nitrates or rat poison lying around!

THE RISK OF POISONING

A cat enjoys exploring and takes an interest in dark, small places where danger can lurk in the form of toxic substances. A cat can occasionally be poisoned by eating or drinking poison, by indirect absorption from eating a poisoned animal, or, more commonly, by licking poison deposited on the fur or paw pads. Similarly, these substances can be absorbed through the skin itself, particularly through the paw pads.

It is vital to keep household cleaning agents in cupboards with catproof doors, and antifreezes and weedkillers safely locked away in garages and tool sheds. Always read the labels of such products carefully; if there are warnings of the danger of the contents to children, they are likely to be bad for your cat too. Although a cat is not likely to choose to drink a bottle of paint-stripper, it could knock

◆ BELOW
This terracotta pot looks safe enough – as long as it does not topple over, and there are no dangerous substances left inside.

◆ BELOW
A cat has taken over the greenhouse. It was allergic to tomatoes, so the plants and all potentially dangerous substances were removed before the cat moved in.

over a bottle containing some. If a toxic substance is spilled on a surface where a cat is likely to tread, mop it up thoroughly. If you are decorating, keep the cat out of the room. Even the smell of modern decorating materials can affect some cats.

Some of the preparations used to keep garden pests at bay are particularly lethal, as they are spread around the garden. Your cat might eat the bird that ate the slug that took the slug pellet, or it just might lick its pads on to which a slug pellet has adhered. So check the contents of any weedkillers, slug bait or growth enhancers and opt for the environmentally friendly varieties. Even these may carry a warning

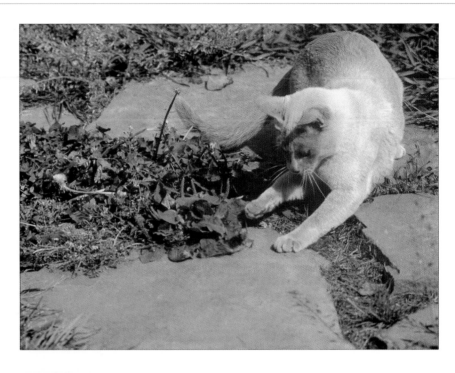

◆ ABOVE RIGHT
The mouse that this young cat is playing with could carry toxins picked up at an earlier point in the food chain.

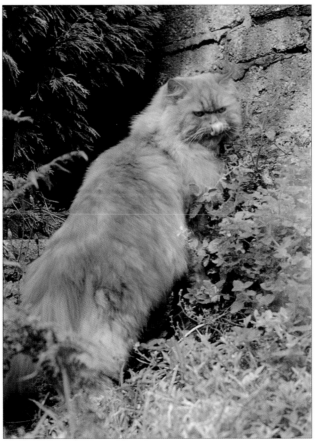

◆ RIGHT
A robust ginger non-pedigree is seeking out some greenstuff to supplement his diet. Most cats instinctively avoid potentially poisonous plants.

regarding domestic pets, and some cats have particular reactions to some substances that are safe for the majority, so keep alert.

Cats usually instinctively avoid the plants which are poisonous to them. However, indirect poisoning could possibly occur if the cat were to eat a bird or a small rodent that had fed on such a plant. Cats do eat grass and other herbage to provide minerals and vitamins, and to act as emetics to get rid of fur balls, for example. Outdoor cats are free to choose their own greenstuff and, because of their normally fastidious nature, seldom make mistakes by taking a mouthful of a toxic plant. Seeds of grasses that are beneficial to cats are marketed, and can be grown indoors. If you do have an indiscriminate plant chewer, avoid having plants that could be dangerous in the house and garden. A garden centre should be able to advise on what these are.

GOING AWAY

Most cats are probably happier to stay in their own homes when owners are away, and there are organizations that will arrange for people to move in and care for your pets. However, this service can be expensive if only one animal is involved. Most people arrange for friends, neighbours, or relatives to live in or to come in regularly to feed and check on the cat. This can sometimes present problems as cats are great individualists, and even if they appear friendly with the sitter when the owners are present may adopt a different view when they have left. In such a situation, a cat might become stressed and stray. It is wise to have a few practice runs and leave the cat for a few days before

risking a two-week break. There is usually no problem with indoor cats, or with outdoor cats that are able to continue coming and going via a cat flap. However, this can be an added worry for the carer, who may prefer the cat flap to be securely locked during the owner's absence. Cats used to freedom might be very keen to escape if suddenly confined in this way. Do make sure, before you leave, that the person who is to look after your cat knows where the cat is and has the keys to all the places to which the cat might have access – the house, the garage, plus any outhouses. Always leave your contact telephone number, and the address and telephone number of your vet, including the emergency service. Discuss responsibilities before you go to ensure that what needs to be done is absolutely clear. Leave written instructions if necessary.

BOARDING OUT

If you decide not to have someone looking after your cat at home, ask your vet for approved local catteries (many veterinary practices have boarding facilities of their own), or ask friends for first-hand recommendations. Do make arrangements well in advance of your departure, as the best boarding catteries may be booked up for months ahead. It is a good idea to visit the cattery before booking to see if the environment and atmosphere will suit your cat. Most prefer you to make an appointment beforehand. There are also questions a boarding cattery

✦ ABOVE
Food, water and a clean litter box are not all a cat wants when its owners are away. Cuddles and games are also important if your cat is not to feel lonely.

✦ LEFT
Being home alone while the owners are away does not present too much of a problem for this cat. It has the freedom of the house, a cat flap for access to outside, and a reliable neighbour to call in and feed it.

◆ ABOVE
This boarding cattery
has outside pens. If
you have an indoor
cat, will it be happy
and warm enough
here?

◆ LEFT
On your preliminary
visit to a cattery you
could check other
residents to see if
they look contented.

BOARDING CATTERY CHECKPOINTS

Points to check on your preliminary visit to a cattery:

◆ are there individual runs?

◆ are the runs and houses inside or outside, and are they are adequately heated?

◆ are the pens sheltered, clean and safely out of the reach of dogs if they are taken in too?

◆ are the beds and bedding disposed of or thoroughly disinfected for each new resident?

◆ are the feeding bowls sterilized between residents?

◆ do the staff seem happy, bright and animal-loving? Do they have any qualifications?

◆ is there plenty for your cat to watch?

◆ do the runs have appropriate sneeze gaps between them? Are the partitions impervious?

◆ are there climbing posts permanently available?

◆ how often are the cats visited during the day?

◆ are the kitchens clean?

◆ is there access to a vet at all times?

owner will ask of you, most importantly whether the cat is in good health and has up-to-date vaccination status. The cattery should have details of your vet's name, address and telephone number, and your own contact address and telephone numbers while you are away. You will be asked for details of special dietary requirements for your cat, and will need to sign a consent form regarding appropriate treatment in the case of illness, and your acceptance of any necessary veterinary bills.

◆ RIGHT
Check there is enough sneezing distance between one pen and another, just in case one inmate develops an infection.

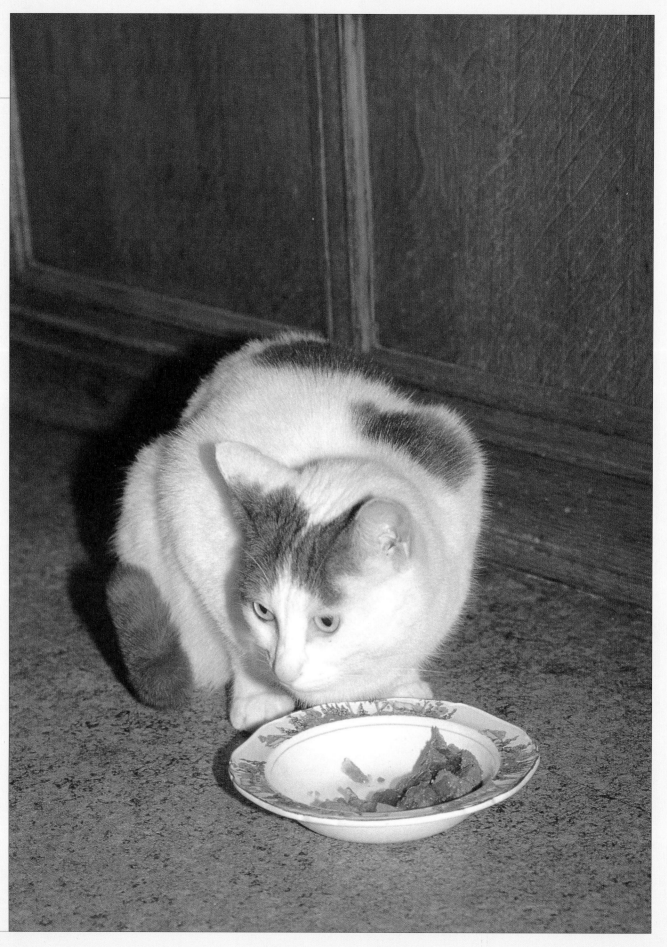

Nutrition and Feeding

If you give your cat a well-balanced diet, it will radiate good health. It will be
contented, alert and active, with bright eyes, a glossy coat and a moist nose.
Regular feeding and a variety of textures and flavours may also contribute to
a contented and healthy cat.

◆ FACING PAGE
Dinner is served on a plate, but if
the owner were to disappear, this
cat would adapt to finding its own
food in the wild.

◆ ABOVE
Two can be company when it
comes to meal-times, as long as
each cat obtains its fair share.

EATING HABITS

✦ BELOW
A cat stalks its prey, a pastime it enjoys and does instinctively rather than being driven by pangs of hunger.

The cat is a carnivore which means that its natural diet consists of the prey which it eats. The cat's teeth and whole dietary adaptation are geared towards the consumption and digestion of entire insects, small rodents, birds, amphibians and fish. While cats do eat some plant matter, they have specific requirements for certain nutrients that can only be found in animal tissues. For this reason, meat must form at least part of a cat's diet. For an owner to try to impose a vegetarian diet would be cruel.

Nutrients are the part of the food that provide energy or raw materials from which the cat builds or replaces its tissues. Unless they are provided in the correct quantity and balance, the cat will not be able to maintain a normal, active life. Nutritional requirements vary at different stages of the cat's life cycle, which is why commercial cat foods are now available for kittens, adults and senior cats. The belief that feeding a cat well makes it less likely to bring its prey into the

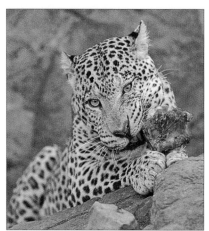

house, or that keeping the cat hungry will make it become a better mouser, is ill-founded. A cat does not need the incentive of hunger to hunt; the healthier it is, the more successful it will be as a hunter.

✦ LEFT
A leopard with its natural prey. Even a domestic cat will appreciate the occasional raw bone.

✦ BELOW
Abandoned kittens enjoy a balanced diet and security at a cat welfare home.

ROUTINE

Feed an adult cat once or twice a day. Serve the food in the same place at around the same time each day. A mixture of canned and dry food is a good idea, for variety, and so that the cat uses its jaws and teeth on the dry food. For the correct quantity, follow the manufacturers' recommendations on the can or packet. An adult 4kg (8lb) cat generally needs around 400g (14oz) of canned food per day or about 50g (2oz) of dry food, depending on its lifestyle. Cats with freedom to roam will need more than an indoor cat, and more may be required during cold weather. Avoid giving snacks between meals. If your cat asks persistently for more, check the quantities are within the above range, but do not feed on a demand basis. If concerned, ask your vet's advice. Overeating and obesity do occur in cats, although to a lesser extent than with dogs. Do not leave food, especially canned food, lying around for long. It dries, begins to smell, attracts flies, and genereally offends the cat's acute senses of smell and taste. Clear away any uneaten food immediately, and wash specially designated utensils and bowls thoroughly. Feeding your cat titbits from the table is not recommended. Cats readily form anti-social habits, and pester you at meal-times.

◆ LEFT
A meal served at room temperature is eaten with gusto. Cold food straight from the refrigerator may be rejected.

◆ ABOVE
A Siamese can persistently ask for more food in a very loud voice. Some indoor/outdoor cats do need more food in cold weather, or simply because they are more active than indoor cats.

◆ RIGHT
A cat takes its meal on a worktop, so that the house dog does not steal its food. Ideally, the area should not be used for human food preparation. A windowsill is more suitable.

A BALANCED DIET

Within its diet the cat requires a balance of proteins, carbohydrates, fats, vitamins, minerals and water. If you give your pet meals at regular times, and offer a variety of fresh and commercial cat foods following the guidelines below, it should get all that it needs without the addition of any dietary supplements such as vitamin pills. Read the labels of commercial cat foods to check the nutritional contents.

PROTEINS FOR STRENGTH

Proteins are made up of amino acids which are the building blocks of the body. They are not only used for growth and repair, but they can be metabolized to provide energy. The amount of protein in a cat's diet depends on its age. As cats become less active with age, they need a less protein-rich diet. In addition, their livers and kidneys have reduced efficiency and are less able to flush out the toxic by-products produced from the body's breakdown of proteins. A kitten, however, because it is growing and building up its muscle mass, needs around 50 per cent of protein in its diet, compared with over 30 per cent

♦ LEFT
Cats enjoy a varied diet and are not averse to raiding the owner's food supplies to achieve it.

♦ BELOW
Natural instinct is the driving force for a cat to hunt, not hunger. Feeding your cat a healthy and adequate diet will not stop it hunting, and could improve hunting performance.

♦ BOTTOM
A pair of Singapura kittens clearly have sufficient animal fats and tissue in their diet to provide them with an abundance of energy.

for a young adult. These levels are around 20 per cent more than those required by a dog of comparable age. The cat's digestive system processes proteins so efficiently that only 5 per cent of total protein absorbed is lost through waste products. Regular ingestion of protein must occur or the cat loses weight and condition. In the wild, feral cats acquire the essential amino acids through a variety of captured animals. Protein-rich foods are meat, fish, eggs, milk and cheese. Today, all nutritional needs are covered in the commercially available, scientifically formulated cat foods.

FATS FOR ENERGY

Fats are the second major source of energy for cats and should form a minimum of 9 per cent of the dry matter of the diet. The cat can digest up to 95 per cent of the fat it consumes; any excess is stored beneath the skin to provide insulation and protection for the internal organs. However, an imbalance between intake and fat used up through normal exercise can lead to an excess of fatty deposits and obesity. Fat is broken down in the body to fatty acids, which are important in the formation and maintenance of cell membranes throughout the body. In addition, fat also provides fat-soluble vitamins to the cat, including vitamins A, D, E and K. Some fatty acids are essential to the cat's diet, and are almost entirely absent from vegetable foods. They come from animal fat and tissue.

CARBOHYDRATES FOR BULK

Carbohydrates are the major energy source for most animals, but the cat can, in fact, survive without them.

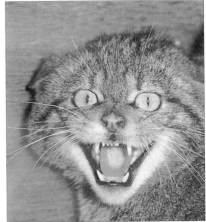

◆ LEFT
The teeth of the wild cat and its domestic descendants are geared to killing and eating small animals. A vegetarian diet would not be appropriate for your cat.

The cat's main natural food sources, birds and mice, are relatively low in carbohydrates, apart from what is found in the stomachs of the prey. However, carbohydrates are a considerably cheaper energy source than protein-rich meat and fish, and are therefore usually incorporated into most commercial cat foods.

Carbohydrates can provide a beneficial boost of readily available energy at times of growth, pregnancy, nursing or stress. They are also a useful source of fibre, which although not digested by the cat, provides bulk in the faeces. A wild cat would obtain fibre from the fur, feathers or stomach contents of its prey, but the domestic cat obtains it from most commercial cat foods in the form of cellulose or plant fibre.

Carbohydrates should not make up more than 40 per cent of the diet.

MINERALS AND VITAMINS

Proteins, fats and carbohydrates are macronutrients, whereas vitamins and minerals are micronutrients – they are required in only small quantities. A cat synthesizes vitamin C for itself, and therefore needs no extra.

Vitamins A, D, E and K work together to refine the bodily functions, and they should all be present in a healthy, balanced diet, together with the vitamins of the B complex. An excess of vitamins can be harmful. Cats fed exclusively on liver, for example (which they love because of the high fat content), may be getting an overdose of vitamin A which is stored in the liver. This can lead to serious arthritic problems involving the legs and spine, even in young cats.

◆ ABOVE AND ABOVE RIGHT
Commercially available snacks, such as these biscuits and milk-flavoured drops, should be given in ones and twos, as an occasional treat, not in bowlfuls as a main meal.

◆ RIGHT
A determined attempt to reach the treats at the bottom of the jar is likely to end in success. It is wise to keep cat-friendly food in sealed containers in cat-proof cupboards if you do not want your pet to help itself at will.

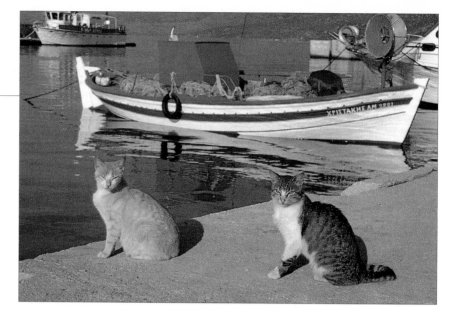

Minerals need to be available in the correct amounts which, in turn, have to be correct in relation to each other. The daily requirements even of macro minerals (which include phosphorus, calcium, sodium, potassium and magnesium) are measured in milligrams (one thousandth of a gram). Trace or micro minerals are also necessary, but daily requirements are measured in micrograms (a millionth of a gram). A cat that has a regular and balanced diet is unlikely to suffer from mineral deficiency, and supplements should not be necessary.

Calcium and phosphorus, for example, are both present in milk, and are very important for the growing kitten. Kittens fed on an all-meat diet and deprived of adequate supplies of milk will develop serious bone abnormalities because they are receiving too much phosphorus (present in meat protein), and not enough calcium. For many years, Siamese breeders weaned their kittens on to a meat and water diet in the belief that milk caused diarrhoea. As a result, bone problems often occurred.

◆ BELOW
A pedigreed cat not interested in its food could be ill or simply not hungry. It may also be bored with the same meal served up yet again and be yearning for variety.

◆ ABOVE
Greek feral cats fend for themselves on the harbourside, their diet of fish supplemented by scraps thrown by tourists from the tavernas.

◆ ABOVE
A raw meat treat for a kitten exercises its jaws, cleans its teeth, and reminds it of its natural diet. It is a good idea to serve it outside!

FOOD SOURCES

You can supplement your cat's canned or dry commercial food for the sake of variety. It is obviously more time-consuming to prepare special meals, but leftovers and scraps can introduce different tastes and textures with minimal effort and preparation. It is essential, however, to have an idea of the benefits and drawbacks of certain foods, and the danger of an unbalanced diet, such as too much liver and vitamin A. If you want to feed your pet exclusively on home-prepared foods, it is advisable to discuss this with your vet, particularly with regard to types, variety and amounts.

FRESH MEAT

A house cat may traditionally have lived off table scraps and odd bits of meat and fish thrown out for it – which probably provided perfectly good nutritional levels. The feral cat will eat a small rodent in its entirety, including bones, innards and muscle and will benefit from all the nutrients these contain.

If you want to feed your cat on raw meat, this must be supplemented with other foods, such as pasta and vegetables for carbohydrates, minerals and fibre, that will provide the equivalent nutritional content of the bones and intestines of the naturally caught rodent.

The best meat, irrespective of type, has a valuable protein content of about 20 per cent. It is best served raw or lightly cooked as many of the vitamins can be destroyed, and the proteins denatured in the cooking process. Protein decreases and fat content increases as the cuts of meat become cheaper. Fat is not a problem, as the cat is well able to digest it and convert it into energy.

Poultry can be served, giblets and all, but make sure the bones are removed, as they become brittle with cooking and could be dangerous. Large pork or lamb bones, however, can provide a cat and kittens with hours of gnawing pleasure and also help to develop jaw strength, keep the teeth clean, and reduce the risk of dental problems in old age. Generally, avoid meats with additives and high salt content such as ham, bacon and sausages. Offal, such as liver and heart, is rich in minerals such as iron, but is also rich in vitamin A, too much of which can cause serious arthritis.

FISH
Uncooked fish has a protein level of over 10 per cent, while fish roes have a high protein level of 20–25 per cent. Raw fish should only be a rare treat, however, as it contains an enzyme that destroys some essential B vitamins. This could result in a variety of symptoms affecting the nervous and gastro-intestinal systems and skin. Oily fish, such as herring or sardines, is highly nutritious and is also higher in fat, making it a better choice than

white fish. A weekly meal of oily fish may help a cat to cope with the fur balls that collect in its stomach, as well as providing fat-soluble vitamins.

VEGETABLES
Cats on a diet of commercial cat food do not need vegetables. Sometimes they eat grass, which is considered to be a natural emetic and possibly a source of minerals and vitamins.

Vegetables are often included in commercial or home-prepared foods as a cheap source of protein and fibre.

DAIRY PRODUCTS
Milk has a useful fat and protein content, as well as lactose (milk sugar), all of which can be beneficial during periods of growth, pregnancy, lactation or stress. Cheese and milk also provide useful minerals such as calcium and phosphorus, but are not part of the cat's natural diet, and should be an occasional treat. Too much can cause diarrhoea, particularly in an older cat. Eggs mashed or scrambled are full of protein and vitamin A, but should never be fed raw as they contain an enzyme that can also destroy some essential B vitamins.

◆ ABOVE
Oily fish, such as pilchards or sardines, are nutritionally better for the cat than white fish.

◆ LEFT
Milk is a nutritious treat, but should be offered occasionally. In an older cat, it can cause diarrhoea.

PREPARED CAT FOOD

Over the last few decades, there has been a tremendous revolution in feline feeding methods. Today there are commercial foods available that cater for all stages of a cat's life. These are available in dry, semi-moist or canned forms, and, in addition, there are deep-frozen foods which come the closest to fresh meat or fish. If the commercial foods are manufactured by reputable, well-known brand names, you can be sure that the contents displayed on the wrapper are balanced. If they are marketed as complete foods, they are complete, and the only necessary addition is drinking water. No vitamins, minerals, or other supplements are necessary. However, cost does increase with quality, and the most expensive varieties are those that are scientifically researched and geared to the dietary needs of cats in each of the three major stages of development: kitten, active adulthood and old age.

Do check the labels for additives (preferably minimal), ingredients and breakdown of nutrient content. Bear in mind, however, that while the average protein content of a can of

◆ ABOVE
Dry food (10 per cent moisture) can be kept longer when opened and left longer in the bowl than wet food, without becoming tainted.

◆ ABOVE
Semi-moist cat food has a moisture content of 40–50 per cent, and so the cat will require less supplementary water than with a dry-food diet.

◆ ABOVE
Canned food (75–85 per cent water) dries and spoils if not eaten immediately. Supplementary biscuits provide exercise for the jaw.

food may be only 6–12 per cent, this is usually the total content per 100g (3.5oz) of food, rather than being calculated on a dry-weight basis. About 10 per cent protein in canned food is equivalent to over 40 per cent dry weight, and is therefore acceptable.

If your cat is fed an exclusively dry diet, fresh water should always be available and changed at least once a day.

WATER
Water is vital for many functions within the body. A cat can survive for 10–14 days without food, but a total lack of water can result in death within days. The daily intake depends very much upon factors such as the moisture content of the food and the climate or temperature. Cats are not great drinkers, and many will hardly seem to drink at all, as they obtain most of their needs from their food. Fresh meat and canned food are made up of about 75 per cent water, whereas dry food contains only about 10 per cent. Because of the domestic cat's evolution from desert dweller (the African wild cat), the kidneys are extremely efficient at conserving water. However, fresh water should be always available, especially if your cat eats dry or semi-moist food.

◆ LEFT
Meat is meat to these two cats; acceptable food has been found, and it will save a great deal of time and bother for their owner if they have the same thing all the time. Some cats appear to demand variety, but it is not essential for good health.

◆ BELOW
It may take six months or more of carefully
controlled dieting to return this obese cat
to a normal weight. Weight reduction in cats
is more difficult than in humans or dogs.

SPECIAL NEEDS

A great deal of research has gone into specialized diets for specific conditions such as heart disease, digestive disorders, lower urinary tract disease, and obesity. If you think your cat needs a special diet, seek the advice of your vet. Most of the diets are only available on prescription.

THE ELDERLY CAT

In young and adult life, cats need protein for growth, to replace worn-out tissues and also as a significant energy source. As cats grow old, they become less active, vital organs start to deteriorate, and their need for protein is reduced.

If you maintain the cat on the same diet it had when it was young and active, there will be an excess of protein. This throws strain on the kidneys and liver, as the protein has to be broken down and eliminated from the body. If the kidneys are not fully functioning due to age, the body tries to maintain the status quo by increasing thirst, and the cat starts to urinate more. This flushes out some of the toxic products, but at the same time removes some essential vitamins and minerals.

Elderly cats in general require a protein level that is reduced from 40 per cent dry weight to about 30 per cent. There needs to be a corresponding increase in fat levels to ensure that sufficient non-harmful energy is available, but not in quantities that might cause obesity. Carbohydrates (such as starches and sugars) should be avoided, as these are more difficult for the elderly cat to digest and can cause diarrhoea and other problems. Sometimes weight loss is noted in an

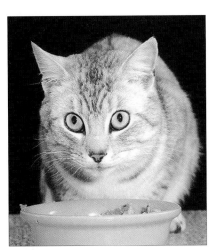

elderly cat even though appetite has not diminished, or may even have increased. In such circumstances, consult your vet, as this may be due to a condition such as hyperthyroidism, which can be treated.

◆ ABOVE
Perhaps its owner has left stale water in the cat's bowl. In any event, the movement of the drips makes this a far more exciting way to drink.

◆ LEFT
An elderly cat's diet should supply easily assimilated protein in the right quantities to sustain energy but not overload the system.

◆ ABOVE
An active adult cat needs – and can assimilate – a higher level of protein in its diet to fuel its lifestyle than an elderly cat.

◆ LEFT
A nursing queen provides everything for her kittens, including the perfect diet, for at least the first three weeks of life.
◆ BELOW
A Brown Burmese kitten has lost its mother, but is not phased by having to join a litter of bull terrier puppies for lunch.

MOTHERHOOD

The first sign of a cat's pregnancy will probably not be a noticeable increase in abdominal size but a demand for more food. If the queen is in good condition at the time of mating, she should not need extra food until about the last third of the pregnancy (seven – nine weeks). By this time the foetuses will be growing in the womb and space is at a premium, so the cat needs frequent small meals, up to four times daily. The total quantity should only be increased by about one third. Top-quality, nourishing food of low bulk is of special importance at this time.

NURSING

To maintain the amount of milk needed for her kittens, a nursing queen will certainly at least double her normal food intake. Food should be of high quality and low bulk – in other words, as much energy and nutrients packed into as small a volume as possible. These requirements are most easily met by some of the special high-energy diets specially devised for nursing queens. Alternatively, kitten food can be used.

THE KITTENS

Kittens suckle from their mother exclusively for the first three or four weeks of their lives. As they become more aware of their surroundings they may start to nibble at their mother's food, a sure sign they are ready for

weaning. The queen will happily continue to nurse her litter to some extent well into their third month of life. However, by the time they are about eight weeks old, the greater part of the kittens' diet will usually be

provided by the owner. There is a fine line between allowing the kittens to gorge themselves, which may cause digestive problems, and giving them enough to maintain healthy growth. The weaning process should be

◆ BELOW
A Burmilla introduces her kitten to grown-up food. Good-quality kitten food will be as nourishing for a still-nursing mother as it is for the growing kitten.

◆ LEFT
The young, active adult cat often cannot last a
whole day before the next meal and will need an
extra snack in-between.

◆ BELOW
A Persian kitten matures over four years and
frequent, nutritious meals need to be given
during this time.

gradual, and the kittens fed little and
often, with small quantities of high-
protein food well chopped so as to be
easily consumable. The easiest method
of weaning is to use one of the readily
available, well-established kitten foods,
either in the dry or canned versions.

During the actual weaning process,
canned foods are probably preferable,
as the kittens may be attracted by the
meaty smell. However, the dry foods
are just as nutritious and have proven
success. Do plan feeding times
carefully so that mother and kittens
may eat the extra meals in peace, away
from other animals or disturbance in
the household.

HOW MUCH, HOW OFTEN?

At about eight weeks old, kittens
should be fed little and often. If you
are feeding dry kitten food (which can
be left out for longer than canned
food), you can try providing it on a
continuous basis for the kitten to
nibble as required. Such a routine
should be avoided, however, if your
kitten shows a tendency to be
overweight. Four or more meals a day
for the kittens is normal, and can be
gradually reduced to about three meals
by the age of three to four months,
and two meals at six months.

THE YOUNG ADULT

The feeding regime can gradually be
reduced to one main meal as the kitten
reaches adulthood at nine to twelve

months of age. However, young,
active cats will become very hungry if
they have to wait 24 hours between
meals. Many owners therefore offer a
snack in the morning, with the main
meal at night. If this is done, it is
important to ensure that the main
meal is reduced in quantity by the
equivalent of the earlier snack, so that
too many calories do not lead to
weight problems. Most breeds of cat
reach their adult size at about a

year of age, although some of the
longhaired breeds continue to develop
until they are about four years old.

If you do have a slow-maturing cat,
it is essential to ensure that adequate
food of high quality is available
throughout the growth period. A
routine of two or three meals a day
with a dry-weight protein value of
over 30 per cent should continue over
the growth period in order to maintain
peak development.

◆ BELOW
These 12-week-old kittens are likely to be
demanding three meals a day.

Grooming

Cats are fastidious animals and devote a large part of their waking hours to grooming themselves. A little extra help from their human friends is required by longhaired and semi-longhaired cats. Even for shorthairs, the grooming process is important. It can be a pleasurable, bonding and rewarding experience for both cat and owner. Extra grooming also contributes to general health, for it stimulates the blood vessels just below the skin and improves muscle tone.

✦ FACING PAGE
A ginger cat uses his paw to clean the parts the tongue cannot reach. The paw stimulates secretions from the glands on the head, which it then transfers to other parts of the body.

✦ ABOVE
A satisfied customer – a Burmese Red – poses for photographs after a grooming session.

THE NATURAL WAY

The cat is well-equipped to groom itself: tongue, teeth, paws and claws are all pressed into service. The cat's tongue has a rough surface which, combined with saliva, helps to remove grit and sticky substances from the fur. Even though cats are very flexible, there are areas they cannot reach directly with the tongue – so the front paws are licked and used rather like a face flannel (washcloth). As the coat dries, the cat nibbles the fur back into place with its small incisor teeth and removes any foreign matter that the washing process failed to dislodge.

The back claws act almost like a wide-toothed comb and remove larger objects from the coat. The front paws stimulate slight oily secretions from glands around the head, and transfer them to other parts of the body during grooming. The cat is preening its coat with its own perfume, which can then be used to mark territory.

◆ ABOVE
A fluffy silver and white kitten shows her remarkable flexibility as she grooms her hind leg. Careful grooming is particularly important with long fur, to remove any matting that could lead to a skin infection.

CHANGING COATS
In the natural state, the cat sheds its coat once a year, usually in spring. However, the process is dependent on light and temperature. In warm, artificially heated and illuminated homes, indoor cats tend to shed throughout the year. It does not happen in one vast shedding of fur, but in discreet areas across the body so that hair loss is hardly noticed – except on the owner's carpets, furnishings and clothes.

When self-grooming at any time of the year, the cat dislodges loose fur, some of which is swallowed. This gradually builds up into a fur ball (hairball) which can eventually solidify into a pellet in the cat's intestine. Most cats automatically bring up a small fur ball every few days or so, but sometimes one can become stuck, causing loss of appetite and a rundown condition. In extreme cases, a vet may need to operate to remove the obstruction. The fur ball problem can strike at any time, although longhaired cats are most at risk. The occasional meal of oily fish may help ease the passage of the ingested hair.

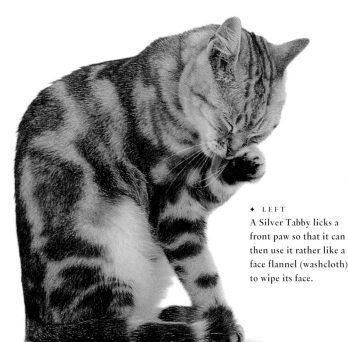

◆ LEFT
A Silver Tabby licks a front paw so that it can then use it rather like a face flannel (washcloth) to wipe its face.

◆ BELOW
The grooming process is completely absorbing for these two kittens. As well as being necessary, grooming is an activity that cats enjoy.

HUMAN AID

A feral cat in good physical condition usually keeps itself reasonably well-groomed. Domestication and selective breeding have resulted in changes to the cat's coat, such as longer hair, that sometimes require more maintenance than the cat is able to provide for itself. Assistance is then needed from the owner. Older cats, too, may lose the motivation and energy to groom themselves and welcome extra help.

You can remove some of the loose dead hairs which accumulate just by stroking a cat. The polishing action gives the coat a beautiful sheen. Some experienced owners claim that the best time to groom a cat is just after washing the dishes, for if your hands are very slightly damp, stroking is even more effective. Thin rubber gloves have a similar effect in removing loose hair.

EQUIPMENT

The grooming equipment you need depends on the type of coat your cat has. You will also gradually discover what works best for your pet. If you have a pedigreed cat, ask the breeder's advice. First-hand experience, especially from a breeder who keeps show cats, can save time and money.

Start regular grooming as a part of a kitten's routine as soon as it comes into your household. An older cat may need some encouragement to submit to the experience, but will probably soon enjoy it immensely, if you are gentle. Choose a quiet time in the cat's observed routine, make sure all you need is accessible and settle the cat on a towel on your lap. It is pointless trying to restrain a cat that just wants to play; scratches are far less likely if the cat is relaxed.

✦ CLOCKWISE FROM BELOW
Narrow/wide-toothed grooming comb, flea comb, ball-tipped brush, slicker tail brush.

✦ LEFT
A longhaired cat is lying down on a towel specially reserved for its grooming. Having a waste (trash) bin nearby is also a wise move.

✦ BELOW
Finish off a grooming session with a stroke and hear that cat purr. Stroking also removes any stray loose hairs and gives a final polish.

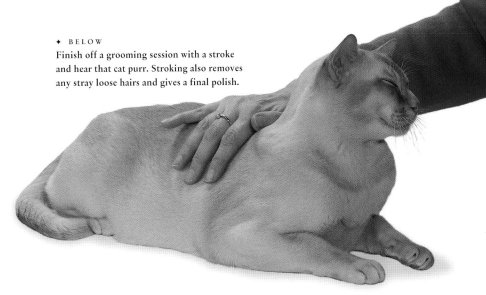

GROOMING A SHORTHAIRED CAT

Supplementing the self-grooming of a
shorthaired cat is really only
absolutely necessary if you are
showing. But an extra groom, say
twice weekly, does help keep loose,
dead hairs under control and off the
furniture. It is also a good opportunity
to check for fleas, or the onset of any
ear or dental problems. In addition,
the activity is pleasurable for both cat
and owner. The process is, of course,
far simpler than for a longhaired cat.
Grooming aids can include a metal

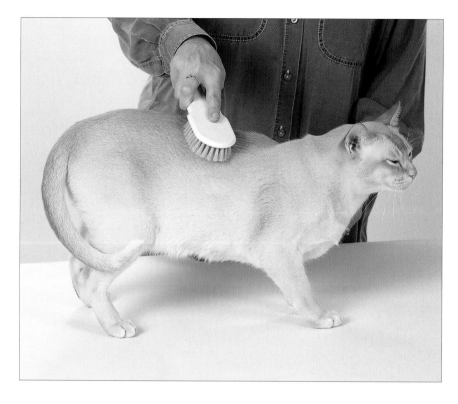

CHECKLIST

- ✦ towel
- ✦ rubber-bristled brush
- ✦ wide-toothed metal comb
- ✦ natural, soft-bristled brush
- ✦ flea comb
- ✦ chamois leather or velvet glove
- ✦ cotton wool
- ✦ ear cleaner
- ✦ eye wipes

comb with round-tipped teeth, a
soft, natural-bristled brush to settle
the fur, a brush with stiffer bristles
(a rubber brush is essential for Rex
cats, as it does not scratch the skin),
and a polishing cloth of silk or
chamois leather. Start the grooming

session by gently stroking the cat
to relax it. Use the stiff brush first,
brushing very gently along the lie of
the fur, to loosen the dead hairs and
dirt. Brush the whole body, but be
especially gentle in delicate parts
around the ears, armpits and groin,

✦ BELOW LEFT AND RIGHT
When grooming is finished, it's time to rest and
watch a friend finish off his tail. Cats often
groom together if they have the opportunity; it
is an important social activity.

✦ ABOVE
A soft-bristled brush settles the fur after any
static triggered by the use of a metal comb.

and under the belly and tail. Next, use the metal comb to extract the dead hairs. It may set up some static in the coat, causing fur to clump together or the guardhairs to develop a wispy life of their own. This will be corrected with the soft-bristled brush, and a final polish with the chamois leather, velvet or silk.

A DRY SHAMPOO

It is rarely necessary to wash a shorthaired cat unless it is a pale-coloured exhibition cat, or unless the cat has become greasy – from sitting under a car, for example. Some exhibitors give their shorthairs a bran bath to remove excess grease, dirt and dandruff. Warm a good five or six handfuls of natural bran flakes in the oven to a comfortable hand-hot temperature. Rub these over the cat, avoiding the face and inner ears, working the hands thoroughly

◆ LEFT
A final sheen is encouraged on a shorthair's coat by stroking it with a chamois leather or velvet glove. A silk scarf would do the job just as well.

through the coat; then simply brush it all out with a soft brush. A coat that is predominantly dark will take on a shine immediately; pastel blues and creams may take a couple of days before their texture and shine reach the peak of perfection.

◆ RIGHT
A contented and very sleek Red Burmese following a full grooming session.

GROOMING A LONGHAIRED CAT

Longhaired cats, whether they are Persians or semi-longhairs – the so-called self-grooming breeds such as the Maine Coon Cat or Norwegian Forest Cat – all need considerable grooming help from the owner. This is true whether the animal is purebred or not. Longhaired cats pick up dirt and debris in their coats, and they need help to keep the fur clean and free from tangles. This must be done daily. If not, the hair mats, particularly in the armpits and groin, and can become uncomfortable. A severely matted coat is unyielding and prevents the cat from moving with ease. Any movement results in individual hairs being pulled. The build-up of fur leads to deterioration in the general condition of the coat and a much greater likelihood of hairballs.

Grooming procedures are more elaborate than for the shorthairs. Start with the wide-toothed comb with blunt teeth to ease out tangles and debris. Try the comb on yourself before you try it out on the cat. If it does not feel sharp on your head, it should be fine for the cat. To deal with obstinate knots and tangles, sprinkle them with unscented talcum powder and ease them free with your hands. A sprinkle of talcum powder also helps pick up excess grease and dirt. It should be brushed out thoroughly at the brushing stage. Make partings in the tail, and brush each parted section sideways. Finish with a well-earned stroke in all the right directions.

1 Use the comb gently to ease out any tangles, knots and twigs. Sprinkle with talcum powder once a week. Do the underbelly and legs first.

2 Brush the body fur firmly in sections against the lie of the fur towards the cat's head. Brush thoroughly to remove talcum powder, if you have used it.

3 Use the fine comb for the neck fur. For Persians, the fur should be combed upwards to form a ruff beneath the chin.

CHECKLIST FOR SHAMPOO AND GROOM

+ towels
+ wide-toothed metal comb
+ fine comb
+ natural-bristled brush
+ unscented talcum powder
+ feline or baby shampoo
+ shower attachment
+ hairdryer

+ RIGHT
A Maine Coon is groomed fit for going on exhibition.

SHAMPOO AND STYLE

Washing a cat is time-consuming, but essential if you are to show your cat. Unless the idea is introduced during kittenhood, a cat may object to being bathed, so it is helpful to have two pairs of human hands.

Make sure the room is warm, free of draughts, and escape-proof. A large, flat-based kitchen sink is ideal. Allow plenty of clear space around the sink, with a stock of dry towels nearby, and one on the draining board. Have all you need at hand before you start.

1 Fill the sink with warm water to about 5cm (2in). Talk soothingly to the cat all the time. Using a shower attachment, test the water first, then wet the fur thoroughly. Apply a little shampoo and work into a lather. Make sure no shampoo goes near the cat's eyes, nose or mouth.

2 Rinse thoroughly and repeat the shampooing process. If you are using conditioner, put a drop on the back and work it through the coat with the wide-toothed comb. Rinse thoroughly and then squeeze down the whole body, legs and tail to remove excess moisture.

3 Lift the cat from the sink and wrap it immediately in a towel. Rub gently to absorb most of the water. You may need several towels!

4 Set the hairdryer on low. Do not direct the airstream too close. Lift and comb the fur as you dry (this is easier if the dryer is on a stand), and stop when the fur is still slightly damp and tacky. If your cat objects to a hairdryer, do not persist, but resort to towels, brushes and patience.

5 Use the soft-bristled brush against the lie of the coat, lifting and brushing as you go. Separate any knots gently with the fingers. Pay particular attention to the flow of the tail plume. Make sure the leg fur is well separated, and that the fur on the underparts, particularly in armpits and groin, does not become curly. On Persians, work up the dramatic ruff of fur around the neck.

ATTENTION TO DETAIL

EYES
The discharges that accumulate in the corners of the eyes can be removed carefully with your finger. Short-faced cats are prone to show tear stains beneath the eyes, which can be cleaned with a special preparation available from pet stores or the vet's surgery.

MOUTH AND NOSE
A dark brown or black tarry secretion on the cat's chin indicates an excess production of sebum from the hair follicles, which is used in scent marking. A similar condition, known as stud tail, can occur around the base of the tail. Veterinary treatment is usually necessary. Recurrence may be prevented by cleansing with special anti-bacterial shampoo from your vet.

TEETH AND GUMS
Keeping your cat's teeth clean reduces the risk of gum disease which has escalated with the advent of modern

◆ **LEFT AND BELOW LEFT**
Daily cleansing of the area around the eyes is particularly necessary with Persian cats. This kitten is being introduced to the idea at an early age. A cotton wool bud (swab) dampened with tepid water is used, and the area is gently wiped with absorbent tissue.

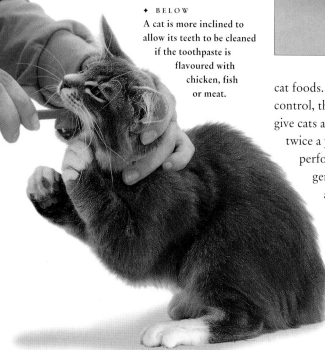

◆ **BELOW**
A cat is more inclined to allow its teeth to be cleaned if the toothpaste is flavoured with chicken, fish or meat.

cat foods. If tartar can be kept under control, the risk is reduced. Some vets give cats a general check-up once or twice a year, and if necessary, perform a scale and polish under general anaesthetic. The alternative is for the owner to clean the cat's teeth once or twice a week. Special toothbrushes that fit over your finger and cat food-flavoured toothpastes make the job easier, but do not necessarily guarantee

◆ **ABOVE**
The owner cleans tartar from the outside surfaces of the kitten's teeth. The cat's rough tongue will take care of any tartar build-up on the inside surfaces of the teeth.

◆ BELOW
A shorthair has its ears checked as part of its grooming routine. A slight build-up of wax means a gentle wipe with absorbent tissue.

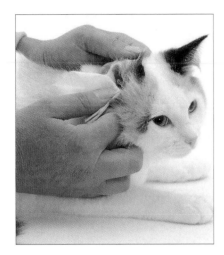

success. Just before feeding time, you could try wrapping a piece of fabric sticking plaster around the index finger. Smear this with a little wet cat food, and gently try to rub against the teeth while holding the head.

EARS
If ears appear soiled on the inside, wipe them out gently with a soft absorbent tissue on your finger, dampened with olive oil, liquid paraffin or ear cleaner from the pet shop. Never clean further than you can see, and do not use cotton wool buds (swabs). An abundance of dark brown, dry waxy material may indicate mites, in which case veterinary treatment is necessary.

CLAWS
Some Siamese cats and their derivatives, such as Balinese, Oriental Shorthairs and Oriental Longhairs, are unable to retract their claws completely and are therefore ill at ease on hard, uncarpeted floors. Elderly cats of any breed may have similar problems. The nails continue to grow and, because older cats take less exercise, are not worn down. Due to stiffness, they are

not fully retracted either. Trimming the nails will help. Outdoor cats should have only their front claws clipped, so that they are not completely disarmed if they meet an enemy, and will be able to climb should escape be necessary.

If claw clipping is necessary, ask the vet to do it, for a mistake could be dangerous. On light-coloured claws, a dark blood vessel can be seen. Cutting

this (called cutting to the quick) causes copious bleeding and pain. Declawing, or onychectomy, is considered an unnecessary mutilation in the United Kingdom. It is widely practised in the United States, and is often carried out at about the same time as sterilization. It is a major operation that removes the cat's main means of self-defence, and should be reserved for indoor cats.

◆ LEFT
A Burmese-cross is having its nails trimmed with a nail clipper custom-made for cats. Clippers designed for human nails may split cats' claws. Only the very edges are trimmed. If you are at all uncertain about your skills, it is wise to ask the vet to do this job.

◆ RIGHT
A thorough self-groom for this cat will help keep fleas and parasites at bay, and in warm weather, help it keep cool. The saliva takes the place of sweat in humans, evaporating and cooling the cat.

Behaviour and Intelligence

The average cat is considered to be fairly intelligent, but compared with dogs its repertoire of party tricks appears paltry. Dogs, as pack animals, will obey understood commands in order to seek the approval of, or a reward from, the owner, who is considered to be the dominant pack leader. The cat is a more solitary animal and may well understand what it is supposed to do but choose not to comply.

◆ FACING PAGE
A kitten practises looking intelligent in front of a mirror. Cats do not have colour vision to the same extent as humans, but they can recognize mental alertness when they see it.

◆ ABOVE
The cat has the body and the build of a hunter – and a temperament and instinct to match.

THE ART OF COMMUNICATION

What a cat is inclined to do and what it can do are quite different. By nature and inclination, for example, cats move gracefully, daintily and sedately, yet their bodies are designed for speed and movement. When establishing a relationship with your cat, bear in mind that it will do what you ask not because it considers you dominant, but because it feels inclined to do so.

A well-balanced cat is used to being handled by its owner, and is alert, independent and inquisitive. If a cat is timid, dependent and constantly seeking attention, it may have suffered misuse or lack of socialization when it was young (6–16 weeks).

LEARNING FROM YOUR CAT

Communication is a two-way process; if you are alert and observant, you will notice subtle nuances in your cat's voice and body language. Listen to your pet in the context of its activity at the time and you may be able to link certain sounds with meanings such as hunger or contentment. Vocalization

♦ RIGHT
A well-balanced cat – confident, alert and relaxed.

and vowel sounds – miaowing – vary from cat to cat. Siamese tend to be very vocal and "talk" to their owners, other cats speak hardly at all. Purring – which can be done breathing in or out and for remarkably long, unbroken periods – is generally an indication of contentment. Kittens start to purr from approximately one week of age; they purr when they are feeding and their mother knows that all is well. It is believed that each kitten has a distinctive and unique

♦ ABOVE
A cat may be comfortably settled on its owner's lap, but its ears remain pricked and alert.

purr so that the queen is able to instantly recognize which of the offspring is communicating.

Fear, anger and dissatisfaction are expressed by spits, hisses and snarls. The pitch of a growl drops when a cat is hunting to become a low hypnotic rumbling. Some cats "chitter" and salivate in anticipation or excitement when they catch sight of something to hunt. Strained, high-intensity yowls are reserved for inter-cat communication, and are especially noticeable in a female on heat.

BODY LANGUAGE

When a cat feels good, its ears are erect and forward-pointing, and its whiskers are relaxed. At rest on a familiar lap, it may purr and "knead" its paws, opening and closing them just as it did against its mother's breast when it was suckling.

If its whiskers bristle forwards, ears turn back, pupils narrow to slits, and fur, particularly along the spine and tail, stands on end, the cat is spoiling for a fight. The fur extension may be accompanied by an arched back so that the cat looks as big and menacing as possible. Wide eyes and flattened whiskers and ears are signs of fear. Whiskers are highly sensitive organs of touch and are sometimes used to make friendly contact with another cat.

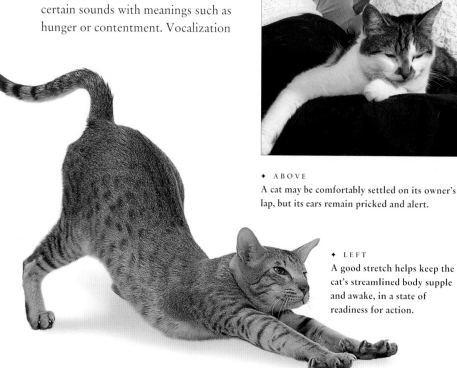

♦ LEFT
A good stretch helps keep the cat's streamlined body supple and awake, in a state of readiness for action.

BASIC INSTINCTS

Cats are nocturnal and may spend up to 16 hours in any one day resting, if not actually asleep. As hunters, they are conserving their energy for the quick bursts of power needed to pursue their targets. Their overwhelming instinct when they go out is to hunt small creatures. This can even be detected in the play of young kittens with toys and leaves. Hearing, sight and smell are geared to the demands of stalking and hunting and these senses are much more acute than they are in humans. Tactile whiskers supplement the other senses, acting as sensors to feel close objects. They may also be used as a friendly whisker-to-whisker gesture with other cats. Cats are sociable and will establish a relationship with other animals or become part of the neighbourhood cat community if they are allowed outside. This community is hierarchical, with the unneutered (unaltered) males and females reigning supreme, and highly territorial.

GENTLE MARKING

Both male and female cats gently assert their territorial rights by rubbing their heads against objects and humans. They leave traces of a scent that is secreted by glands located at various parts of the body, but particularly around the ears, neck and at the back of the head. The scent is also released from between the paw pads when a cat scratches a tree to sharpen its claws.

◆ ABOVE
As this cat rubs its forehead against a chair, a scent is released that proclaims the chair as part of the cat's own territory.

◆ ABOVE
At still only a couple of weeks old, this kitten has not begun to acquire trust or domesticated patterns of behaviour; it is still in its feral state, expressing fear and aggression at intruders.

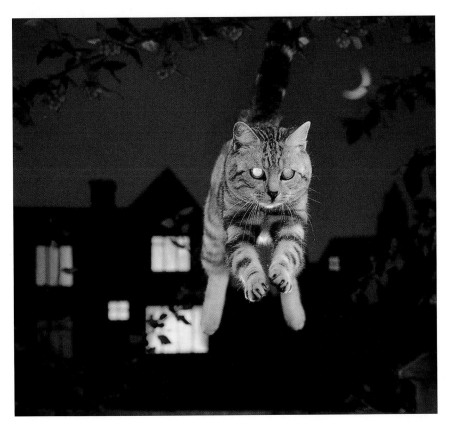

◆ LEFT
A cat pounces. Its specially adapted eyes, with their wide angle of vision, are able to make the most of limited light, enabling a cat to detect the slightest movement in dim light.

TERRITORIAL RIGHTS

The cat instinctively carves out a social and hunting territory for itself. This behaviour is most marked in the unneutered (unaltered) male, whose main purpose in life is to pass on his genes to future generations. He may extend his territory to cover an area of as much as 10km (7 miles), maintaining his position in the social hierarchy and priority access to any local females by fighting. His life can be violent and short.

An unneutered female can fight as effectively and as viciously as the tom, as she develops and defends her hunting territory. From about four months of age, she periodically attracts all the males in the neighbourhood and regularly becomes pregnant.

DOMESTIC IMPLICATIONS

For the domestic neutered (altered) cat, its own home and garden are the focal points of its territory. An unneutered cat will extend the area

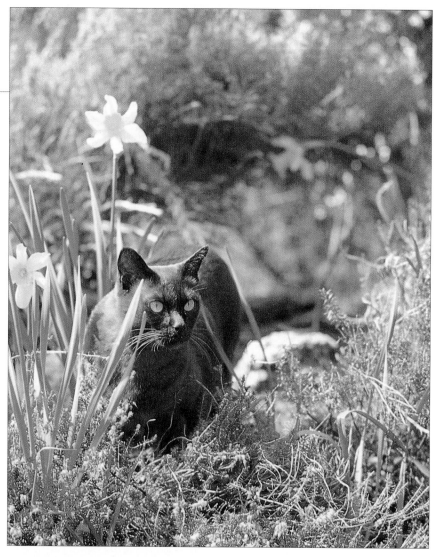

and challenge the neighbourhood cats. Kittens that are brought up together usually co-exist happily unless there are too many cats in the household, which could result in some territorial marking. If an adult cat is introduced into a home where there are cats already, care and sometimes expert guidance is needed. Among neutered cats, territorial rights may be resolved by some violent vocals, body language, and the establishment of non-violent dominance. If the cats are unneutered, it is a different story.

SPRAYING

The cat marks the boundaries of its patch with a spray of concentrated, very strong-smelling urine. It will also

✦ ABOVE
A cat sprays to mark the boundaries of what it considers to be its territory. If the cat – whether male or female – has been neutered, the smell is unlikely to be obvious to humans.

✦ LEFT
Two cats demonstrate their affection for each other by rubbing their foreheads together. Other signs of friendship may include licking each other or brushing whiskers.

♦ OPPOSITE
A male Burmese goes hunting: it could roam as far as 10km (7 miles) in search of food and female company if it is not neutered.

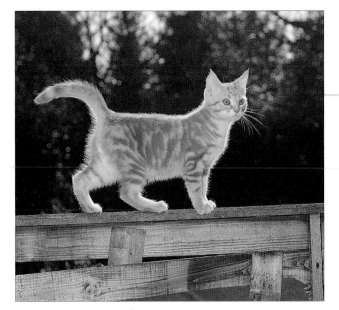

♦ BELOW
Son, aged six months, is keen on keeping close to his mother. The dominant, unneutered female, however, is not always this complacent, and often asserts her independence.

♦ RIGHT
A kitten begins to explore outside, ready to take its place among the local community and hierarchy of cats.

do this if it feels threatened or insecure, for example, if strange visitors or animals come into the house. The most common and the most pungent spraying comes from unneutered males, but entire females spray, especially when they are on heat. Neutered cats also spray, but the odour is usually less offensive.

In extreme situations, the marking may involve dropping faeces away from litter trays (pans). This is not simply dirty behaviour, but dysfunctional, and the causes must be established. A cat that constantly re-marks its territory is trying to reassure itself that it is worth something. The wise owner checks with the vet for medical advice. Home treatment of attention and affection may solve the problem. If the behaviour continues, you may be referred to an animal behaviourist.

THE EFFECT OF NEUTERING
Neutering (altering) dramatically reduces a cat's urge to exert territorial rights. Territory becomes confined to

an area around the home (although this will still be robustly defended by a neutered cat of either sex).

In a neutered, or castrated, male, the means of producing the hormones that fuel sex drive – the testes – are removed. Castration takes place ideally from four months of age. It is done under general anaesthetic. No stitches are needed, recovery is complete within 24 hours, and there is no discernible traumatic effect on the cat. Long-term, however, the animal's territorial, sexual and hunting behaviours are modified. A female is

neutered or spayed by the removal of her ovaries and uterus, or womb, so that she cannot become pregnant. She no longer comes on heat or attracts all the local males. The operation is ideally carried out from four to five months of age. Once the cat has recovered from the anaesthetic, she is usually fine. Long-term she may become more friendly and placid. Desexed animals do tend to convert their food more efficiently, and may be less active. If they start to look plump, some attention to diet may be necessary.

♦ RIGHT
Two neutered (altered) Burmese, who have known each other since kittenhood, are happy to share their limited territory of house and garden amicably.

BEHAVIOURAL PROBLEMS

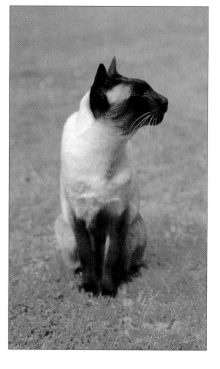

It is sometimes difficult to recognize symptoms of stress in the solitary, individualistic feline. Some breeds are more nervous than others. Highly strung Orientals, for example, can react very badly to strange situations, and even the first visit to a cattery may change the personality. Stolid domestic shorthairs may be equally upset, but are more likely to react aggressively – by hissing, scratching and biting. Cats probably show stress to a greater extent than dogs, but the first signs are sometimes too subtle for us to notice.

SYMPTOMS OF STRESS

When feeling vulnerable, a cat withdraws into itself, and cold aloofness is one of the first clues to its condition. A cat about to go into battle tries to appear as large as possible, but in distress it tries to become mouse-sized. Fur is flattened, tail is curled round and the cat crouches. If the situation continues, the cat starts to shake. Salivation, vomiting and defecation can also be signs of nervousness and tension.

A cat may react actively or passively when it is frightened. Typical, active signs are pupil dilation, arching back, piloerection (the hair stands on end) and hissing. A cat may react to any attempts at reassurance, such as vocal intonations or body contact, with further aggression.

Passive symptoms of fear are more subtle and harder to detect. The cat may hide or try to appear smaller, placing the ears back and becoming immobile. A timid cat will start at the slightest movement or unexpected noise.

This may be because it was abused as a kitten, or simply because it lacked proper socialization. If you breed, it is important to socialize your kittens to prepare them for everyday household life and noise.

DEALING WITH FEAR

Mild fear may be overcome by the owner. A timid cat needs a safe, quiet place to retreat to, such as a covered bed. Avoid forcing your attentions on the cat – wait for it to approach you. Always move slowly, speak to it softly and evenly and keep strangers or strange situations at bay until it has become more confident.

It is important to identify the cause of a cat's fear so that you can deal with it. This may not always be easy, unless

✦ ABOVE
An aggressive cat seeing off an unwanted visitor. Neutering makes a cat more placid.

✦ LEFT
A timid cat crouches or hides when feeling threatened by the slightest noise or an unexpected situation.

it is obvious – a one-off visit to the vet, for example. There may be an ongoing situation, such as mild teasing behaviour by a child, or persistent noise or confinement. Once the cause is established, it must be removed and the cat's confidence regained.

It may be that you can persuade the cat to overcome its fears. Cats have a highly developed flight response and when faced with any threatening situation, such as being trapped in a carrier or a car, their immediate reaction is to try to get away. You may be able to control this with soothing words or by gradually making the cat realize it needn't be afraid by exposing it little and often to the situation.

After an initial shock reaction, cats often settle down in catteries or veterinary hospitals after about 48 hours. If they are handled, however gently, during that time, they may

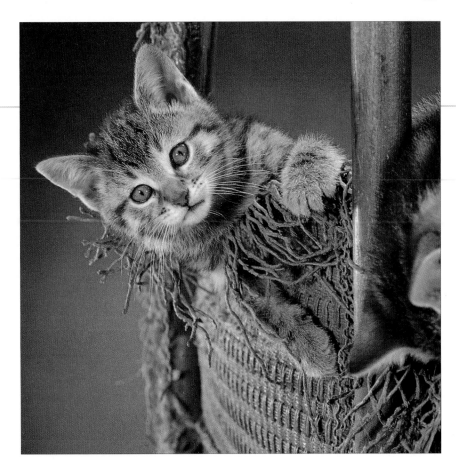

associate the handling with the initial fear and bridle every time anyone approaches to feed them. Left alone, they usually calm down and soon start to make overtures to the very people that they hated the day before.

DEALING WITH AGGRESSION

If a cat that is normally calm and well-behaved suddenly starts to scratch and bite, it may be ill, bored or frightened, and the underlying cause should be addressed. It is important to train a kitten from the beginning that aggressive behaviour is unacceptable, even in play. A firm no, immediate cessation of play, and a light tap on the nose whenever it bites or scratches should correct this behaviour. Do remember that a cat likes its independence, and if you impose your attentions on it when it does not want them – for example, if it is asleep – it may react instinctively by attacking you.

◆ ABOVE
Scratching is fun for the kitten, but does not do the soft furnishings much good. Provision of a scratching post and a little training should solve the problem.

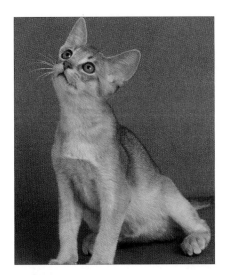

◆ ABOVE
A kitten in listening mode. It is important to talk encouragingly to your pet when it has behaved well, and never shout at it or hit it. A firm, quiet "no" and a tap on the nose should be sufficient to stop any mischief.

◆ ABOVE
Play with your indoor cat as often as you can to ensure it gets enough exercise and attention, or its boredom could turn to destructive tendencies.

TRAINING AND LEARNED BEHAVIOUR

Switched-on, intelligent cats will soon learn to manipulate doting owners. They can also be trained to produce predictable repeatable behaviour. The degree of training depends very much on the amount of time the owner has to spend with the cat. A kitten's play is, in fact, its instinctive means of acquiring hunting and survival skills.

Although many hunting actions are instinctive, they are also learned from other cats. Solitary, hand-reared kittens do not learn to hunt.

Each kitten is an individual with a unique temperament and balance of skills. In encouraging and extending a kitten's play, you can observe the strengths and weaknesses in its temperament and skills repertoire. Observing and enhancing natural

◆ LEFT
A Bi-colour Ragdoll kitten has retrieved a toy. It may take it back to its owner for it to be thrown again.

traits is the secret behind the methods of successful animal trainers. All cats show skill at balancing and spacial awareness, but some are much better than others. A kitten may pick up a piece of crumpled paper and bring it to its owner to be thrown again. You can encourage repetition of this trick with a tasty titbit and pretty soon you will be boasting about your "retriever" cat!

You can train your cat to conform to certain household standards, using spoken commands which the cat is well able to understand and respond to.

ESTABLISHING COMMUNICATION

The first step in training is to establish communication between cat and human, and a kitten should be given a name as soon as possible. If an adult cat joins the household, it is advisable to retain its existing name even if you dislike it. If you use the cat's name repeatedly when you are attracting its attention, it will soon learn to respond. From there it is easy for the cat to learn certain command words. Repetition of the verbal message, spoken firmly in a low voice, and

◆ LEFT
Each kitten is an individual with its own strengths, weaknesses and special skills. This kitten's speciality seems to be acrobatics.

◆ RIGHT
Kittens and young cats enjoy playing hide-and-seek – as long as they are found quickly, congratulated and cuddled.

◆ LEFT
The intelligent cat helps
itself to a treat.

best sofa, say no, gently but
firmly, take it to the
scratching post, and place its paws
on the post. If the cat uses the post,
give it some praise and a stroke.

USING THE CAT FLAP
Practice and encouragement is also the
key to training a cat to use a cat flap.
Make sure the door is at a comfortable

◆ ABOVE
To dissuade a cat from nibbling your
houseplants, provide it with its own pot of cat
mint. You could also try wiping the leaves of
plants you want to protect with a solution of
lemon juice and water.

never shouted, is the key. Avoid
shouting, for this can traumatize a cat
and lead to behavioural problems.

SAVING THE FURNITURE
A cat scratches a tree – or your
furniture – to sharpen its claws, to
mark its territory, or just for the
satisfying feeling. If you want to
conserve your furniture, therefore,
provide your cat with a scratching
post, and, as an extra incentive, rub
some catnip into it. Whenever the cat
begins to assault the curtains or the

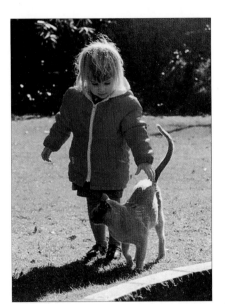

◆ LEFT
A cat enjoying the companionship of its young
owner. Although independent, most cats are
social animals and prefer to have company.

height for your cat and that the
flap swings easily. Place some
tempting food on the far side
of the door and gently push
the cat through. Then open
the flap slightly and call the cat back.
Repeat a few times and the cat will
soon learn to operate the flap itself.

◆ ABOVE
Here's a positive response to an owner's call.
From the look of expectancy and the line of the
tail, it is probably supper time.

◆ LEFT
Boy and kitten play
together. This is
important for both –
the child learns to be
gentle and kind to
animals. The kitten
does not become lonely
or bored and hones its
hunting techniques.

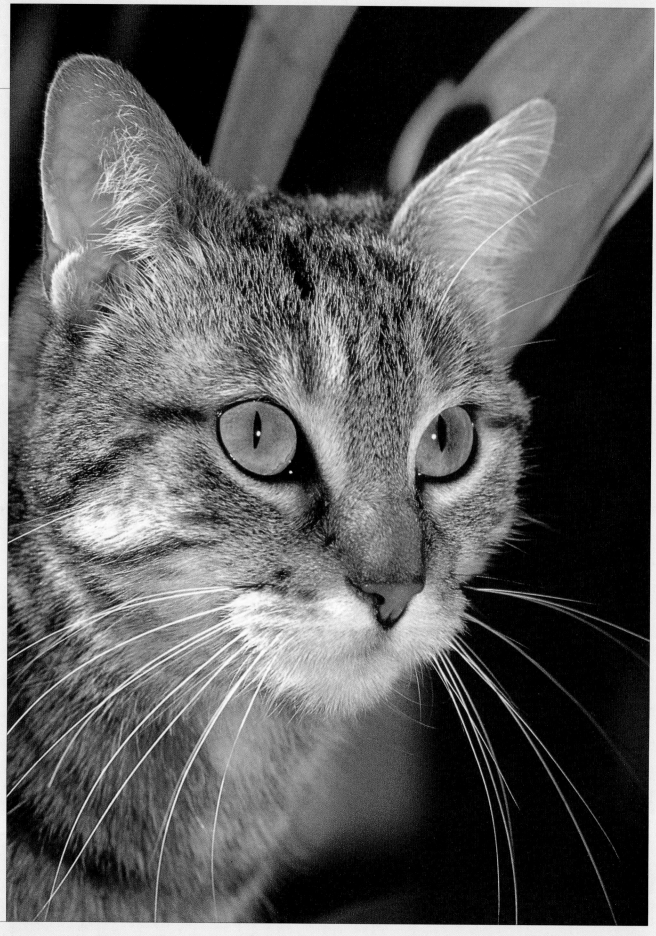

General Care and Everyday Health

A cat is a survivor, and if it is injured, will often keep going regardless, making it difficult to spot if anything is wrong. Getting to know your cat's character, giving it regular checks, and understanding a little about the strengths and weaknesses of its body will help alert you to the first signs of illness or injury. Vigilance and care will keep the vet's bills down, too. If an emergency arises, knowing how to deal with it may save your cat's life and increase its chances of a full recovery.

◆ FACING PAGE AND RIGHT
Two images of cats in prime condition. Bright eyes, alert expressions and a proudly carried tail are all indicators of sound physical and mental health.

HOW TO TELL IF YOUR CAT IS SICK

The cat's coat is a barometer of health. It reflects the quality of its diet and general condition, and should be gleaming and free from dandruff. The healthy cat's eyes are bright and clear with no discharge, redness or blinking. The tissue around them is pale pink in colour rather than red and inflamed. Nose leather is cool and slightly moist from the cat's tear ducts, and licking also keeps the nostrils moist.

Often, it is only by knowing your cat and understanding how it normally behaves, looks and reacts within its usual environment that you can tell if anything is wrong. You are the mirror of your cat's health, so do not be afraid to mention anything abnormal that you have noticed, no matter how small. The vet may only see your cat once a year and does not know its normal character or behaviour. Particular points to look out for are changes in eating or drinking habits.

SIGNS OF A SICK CAT

The first sign that your cat is not well may be a change in its normal behaviour or appearance that may only

✦ ABOVE
A Red Tabby is interested in the life going on around it, as every healthy cat should be.

✦ ABOVE
An alert expression, pricked up ears and a glossy coat suggest that this cat has a balanced diet and a healthy, contented life.

✦ LEFT
A cat playing is in character – if it were suddenly to become uninterested in playing and listless, this would be a sign to the owner of possible ill health.

WHEN TO CALL THE VET

If your cat is displaying any of the following symptoms, call the vet immediately:

✦ blood in vomit, urine or faeces

✦ excessive thirst

✦ swollen and tender abdomen

✦ high temperature

✦ vomiting and diarrhoea together

✦ bleeding from penis or vulva

✦ straining when it tries to pass urine

✦ shallow, laboured breathing

✦ after a road accident

---

be perceptible to you. If a normally friendly cat shows signs of aggression, or an outgoing animal suddenly becomes withdrawn, timid and shy, look for other signs of illness. Lack of response to being called may be due to fever or temporary deafness caused by ear mite infestation.

COAT

A stary, ungroomed look to the coat with abnormally raised fur is a general indication of ill health.

STOOLS

If you still have cause for concern, check the cat's stools: they should be firm and without extreme or pungent odour. If you have an outdoor cat, confine it if possible and provide a litter box, so that you can make this check.

Where cats have access to dustbins, diarrhoea may be caused by a stomach upset resulting from eating contaminated food, but could be a sign

UNDERSTANDING YOUR CAT'S ANATOMY

The cat's skeleton provides support and protection for the vulnerable, internal organs. The entire feline skeleton is strong but light, as befits its function as a hunter.

The coat normally comprises a dense, soft undercoat covered by coarser hairs which are known as guardhairs. The density of the fur adds further protection to the skin (epidermis) from which it grows.

Skin consists of many layers of cells. These are constantly reproducing to compensate for the loss caused by sloughing of the cells which die and are shed from the surface as scurf.

TAIL Tail bones are joined by a complex machinery of small muscles and tendons, making the tail capable of a great range of movement. This enhances balancing potential and has also developed as a barometer of the cat's emotional state.

EYES Deep, large eye sockets facing forward protect the eyes. Binocular vision gives the depth of focus needed by a hunting animal in order to judge distances accurately.

HEAD is that of a typical predator, with a strong skull protecting the brain. It is capable of a wide range of movement due to the very flexible neck.

EARS Large, cup-like outer ears collect a vast range of sound. This is helped by tiny muscles which give the ears great flexibility of movement. The inner ear assists with balance.

BACK The back muscles are well developed to allow the cat to carry heavy weights over long distances. The spinal column ranges from the closely positioned bones of the chest to the longer, heavier lumbar vertebrae which support the weight of the body organs.

PELVIS is fused to the vertebrae of the lower back, and these are also linked to the progressively smaller bones of the tail.

TEETH are those of a typical predatory carnivore – canine teeth, or fangs, for killing; incisors for gripping; heavy, sharp molars for chewing and tearing. This process is helped by a very flexible lower jaw arrangement which allows sideways movement so that the tearing process becomes very efficient.

FRONT LEGS are capable of some rotation so that the pads can be presented to the face, for use in the washing process.

PAWS are long so that the cat actually walks on its fingers and toes which are supported by the sensitive fleshy pads. Claws are capable of being retracted.

BACK LEGS Movement is restricted to backwards and forwards only. The way in which the knee opposes the position of the elbow at the front, allows for the enormous spring which gives the cat the ability to pounce.

of something more serious, especially if it is persistent. Constipation, causing the cat to strain, can also be a problem, especially if there is any blood in the stools.

EYES

If the third eyelid – the haw or nictitating (blinking) membrane – is visible, it indicates an infection or that there is a foreign body in the eye. Any signs of redness or inflammation or excessive and persistent, thick, yellowish discharge are cause for concern. If either pupil appears dilated or does not react to bright light, this needs prompt veterinary attention.

EARS

Clear wax in the ears is normal, but a dark brown waxy deposit may indicate ear mites that need veterinary treatment. Look out for seeds, such as grass seeds, too. A seed may lodge in the ear and enter the ear canal, making the cat shake and scratch its ear. The wall of the ear canal and flap (pinna) is

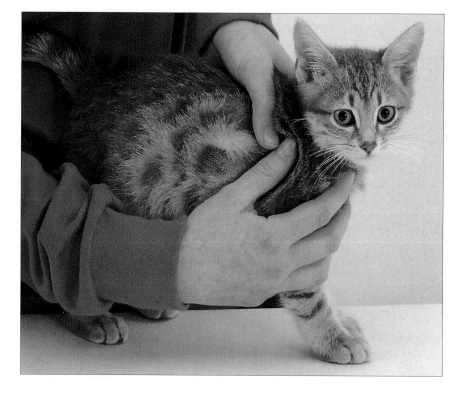

extremely delicate and vulnerable to damage in fighting situations. A puncture to the pinna often results in a haematoma (a large blood blister) that could become infected if not

treated. If the ears are very hot, the cat may be running a temperature, but before rushing to the vet, check this is not due to your cat lying in the sun or next to a radiator!

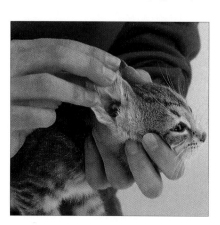

✦ ABOVE
An owner gently holds back the ear to check that there are no scratches on the pinna (the inner lining of the outer ear). Also check for dark, waxy deposits.

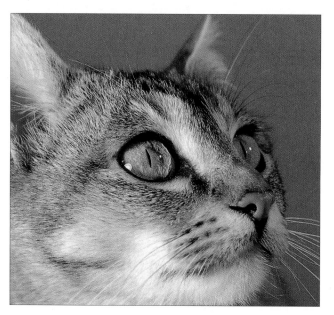

✦ ABOVE
As part of the regular care routine, make a random check in the fur by parting it until you can see the skin.

✦ LEFT
As in humans and other animals, the state of a cat's eyes can indicate problems elsewhere in the body. This cat's eyes are those of a radiantly healthy animal.

♦ RIGHT
It is important to check the cat's third eyelid, or nictitating membrane. If this shows on its own, it suggests there is something wrong. The cat may have an infection or a foreign body in its eye.

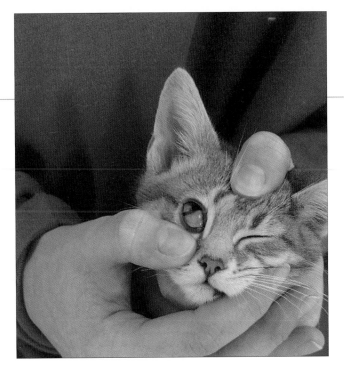

SICKNESS

Light vomiting is very often no cause for alarm. It may be due to the cat having bolted down its food too fast, a reaction to something it has caught and eaten, to grass that it has chewed to clear its system out, or a physiological response to remove hairballs. Persistent vomiting, however, especially if it contains any blood, is important, and is reason enough to check with the vet.

TEMPERATURE

A good indication that the cat has a raised temperature is if the ears feel hot. A rectal thermometer is needed in order to take a precise temperature reading, which should be 38–38.5°C (100.5–101.5°F). Unless you have been taught how to do this properly, it is best left to a professional.

PULSE

Key pulse points in a cat are located under the forearms (armpits) and back legs (groin). The pulse rate may vary between 120 and 170, depending on how active the cat has been recently. The average is 150.

REGULAR CHECK-UPS

The caring and wise owner checks the pet regularly to make sure it is in top condition. Early signs of conditions such as mite infestation or fleas will prevent more serious problems developing later. The check-up can be at a time when you are relaxing with your cat, or if it is one that needs regular grooming, as an integral part of the grooming routine. If a cat does show any signs of ill-health or

♦ ABOVE
Modern cat food does not give a cat's teeth the exercise and cleaning power that would come from hunted food. It is therefore important to check them regularly.

discomfort, you can go through the checking points described on the previous pages. Then, if you do need to take it to the vet, you can give a detailed report on anything unusual you have noticed.

FUR AND BODY

One good reason for grooming your cat regularly, even if it is a shorthair, is that you will be quickly alerted to any lumps, or signs of attack by fleas, ticks, mites or lice. If the grooming process rakes out some grit-like dirt, check further. Comb the cat over moistened absorbent paper. If the grit leaves a red stain, these are the blood-gorged faeces of fleas. If not, the cat has just been rolling in the garden.

Small, raised grey or whitish lumps indicate ticks. These can irritate the cat considerably as the tick's head is buried deep into the skin, leaving only the body visible. They should be removed as soon as possible but great care has to be taken to ensure that the head is removed as, if left behind, an abscess or sore can develop.

EARS, NOSE AND MOUTH

Check that ears are clean and free of dark waxy deposits and seeds. Even minor scratches need to be kept clean to prevent infection. Check for broken or discoloured teeth, swollen gums and bad breath, and make sure there are no lumps (enlarged glands) around the neck.

PAWS

The claws of an indoor cat need to be checked regularly in case they need clipping and to prevent them from ingrowing. Also check for any soreness or wounds on the pads.

HOME NURSING

A sick cat should be confined in an area that is warm and free from draughts, quiet and capable of being easily cleaned and disinfected. The first two requirements are relatively easy to fulfil, whereas the third could cause some problems. Many modern homes are carpeted throughout which makes disinfecting difficult. If there is not a separate utility room with a floor that is easily cleaned, you should consider buying a large, plastic travelling carrier which comes apart so that every part can be thoroughly cleaned.

Use a disinfectant agent recommended by your vet – it is most important to avoid any substances containing coal-tar, wood-tar, phenol, cresol and chloroxylenols. These

◆ LEFT
Special syringes, available from your veterinary practice and some pet shops, will help you administer medicines.

◆ BELOW
A warm, comfortable bed and plenty of tender loving care are essential when nursing a sick cat.

agents are fine for use with people but can be lethal for cats. If a condition is seriously infectious to other cats, you should set aside some old clothes and shoes to wear when handling the sick cat, and wash thoroughly afterwards. Always dispose of any used bandages or applicators promptly. Thoroughly clean up any vomit or faeces without delay and disinfect the area carefully.

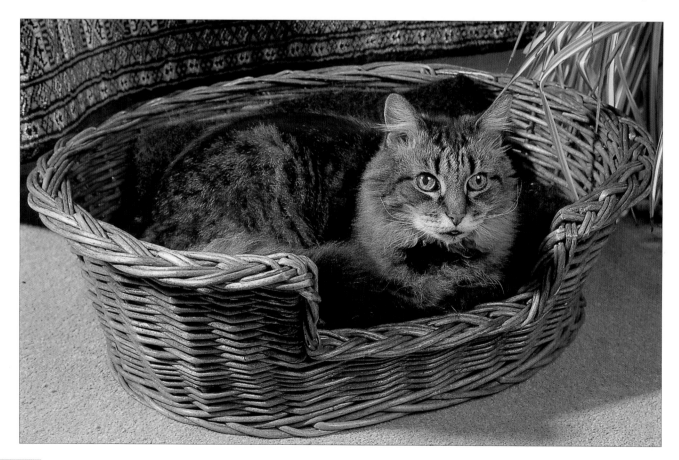

BEDSIDE MANNER

You can help your cat's recovery tremendously with care, love and attention. Spend time talking quietly, maintaining appropriate physical contact without being overwhelming, and ensuring that its bodily needs are catered for. The cat may not be able to do anything for itself and, therefore, feeding, watering, grooming and assisting with toilet procedures become your responsibility. While this is very time-consuming, the bond you have already achieved with your cat will grow even stronger. The veterinary nurses (technicians) will help if you need advice on the various techniques involved with the grooming, feeding and toileting of a sick cat.

ADMINISTERING MEDICINES

Your vet will always give advice and instruction on how much and how often you should administer any medication your cat needs for treatment. Medicinal preparations come in several forms – liquids, pills, capsules, drops and lotions. The secret of administering any of these

successfully and with least disturbance to the animal is to have confidence in your ability to do so. However, some cats will object tooth and claw to having any foreign object forced into their mouths. If this is the case with your cat, you will need to ask someone to assist you and, if necessary, wrap the cat securely in a towel to help immobilize it.

Liquid medicines can be given using a plastic syringe obtainable from your vet or from most pet shops. After use it should be cleaned thoroughly and then stored for future use in a sterilizing agent such as one of those used for baby feeding equipment. Draw up the amount for one dose into the syringe. Holding the cat's head firmly, gently insert the syringe between the lips, at the side of the mouth. Push the plunger gently so that the cat receives the dose slowly and gradually, allowing it time to swallow. This reduces the risk of any liquid going into the lungs, which could cause pneumonia to set in rapidly in the case of a sick cat. Pill poppers which look like elongated syringes are available if you have

difficulty opening your cat's mouth. The pill is placed into the popper and a plunger pushes the pill to the back of the cat's tongue. Direct the instrument towards the palate rather than pressing on the tongue. Hold the cat's mouth closed and stroke its throat until it has swallowed.

DROPPING IN

Most preparations designed to be dropped into the eyes or ears are supplied with a dropper or a dropping nozzle. If not, droppers can be purchased from chemists (drugstores). Always carefully read the directions about how and when to apply the medication, before using.

The membranes of the eyes and ears are very delicate and it is most important for the cat to be held securely. Another pair of hands makes the job much easier.

With eye drops, one drop is usually sufficient. For ear drops, hold the pinna (ear flap) firmly to open the canal, and place two or three drops into the ear, then massage gently. Ear drops are usually oily and overdoing the drops results in a greasy head.

ADMINISTERING TABLETS

1 Hold the cat's head firmly, with your fingers on either side of the jaw, and gently pull the head back until the jaws open.

2 Talking quietly and encouragingly to your cat throughout the process, drop the pill or capsule at the back of the cat's tongue.

3 Hold the mouth closed and massage the throat until a swallowing action shows that the pill or capsule has been ingested.

ACCIDENT AND INJURY

Emergency treatment is often required for accidents within the home. Do not assume that a cat or kitten will automatically know its physical limits or be able to tell, for example, which plants are poisonous. It might well be able to fall from any angle and regain its footing, but only within certain heights. A cat falling from a balcony is just as likely to sustain serious damage as any other animal. Cats can be as vulnerable to accidents as children, and you should keep a constant eye on safety in your home.

It is valuable to know what on-the-spot treatment you can give before the cat receives veterinary attention. In extreme situations, this could make the difference between life and death. A cat that is very frightened or in pain may instinctively withdraw, and scratch and bite if handled. If this happens, talk calmly and keep the cat as warm, comfortable and confined as possible until professional help is available. As with any emergency, the first rule is not to panic and the second is to rely on your common sense. However inexperienced, you will learn by careful observation to recognize the real emergency. Prompt first aid is all that is needed, but if you are in the least doubt about the seriousness of any condition, seek professional help immediately. All veterinary practices have to offer a 24-hour emergency service. Phone the surgery number first to check for any special emergency arrangements, or at least to give the surgery advance warning of your imminent arrival.

A cardboard box is a good carrier in an emergency; if an injured cat is placed on a board serving as a stretcher, it could easily fall off. Keep the cat warm by covering with a blanket and call the vet immediately. Try not to panic and handle the cat as gently as possible.

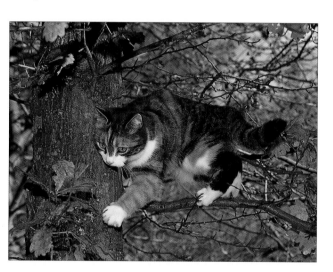

◆ LEFT
A cat is so intent on stalking a moving leaf or insect that it may end up on a branch that cannot support its weight and fall.

WHEN TO WORRY

◆ obvious or suspected injury from a fall (usually 4m/12 ft, or more), or from a road traffic accident

◆ obvious fractures or dislocations

◆ profuse bleeding

◆ choking or respiratory distress

◆ severe burn or scalding

◆ collapse or a fit lasting more than a few seconds

◆ injuries to or foreign body in the eye

THE FIRST-AID KIT

◆ sterile pads and dressings

◆ bandages: 2.5cm and 5cm (1in and 2in) widths

◆ stretch fabric adhesive strapping

◆ lint padding or cotton wool roll

◆ cotton wool balls (uncoloured)

◆ antiseptic wipes, cream and lotion (as recommended by your vet)

◆ small, blunt-ended scissors

◆ tweezers

◆ nail clippers

◆ non-prescription soothing eye drops

◆ ear cleaner

◆ liquid paraffin

◆ kaolin mixture

◆ antihistamine cream

◆ rectal thermometer

◆ water-based lubricant

◆ eye dropper

◆ 5ml (1 tsp) plastic syringe

◆ sterilizing agent

◆ Elizabethan (medical) collar

◆ surgical gloves

◆ suitable carrier or box

IMMEDIATE ACTION

What should you do in an emergency? If the cat is in a situation where further injury could occur, such as a busy road, move the animal carefully. Depending on the position of the injuries, try to grasp the cat gently by the scruff and support its weight with the other hand. Put it in a suitable box or carrier. If the cat is unconscious, take precautions against choking by clearing any blood or vomit from the mouth and pulling the tongue forward. The head should be below the body level when the cat is lying down so that any fluids can run out.

If there is severe bleeding try to stem it by putting a pressure bandage (like a tight bandage) over the wound. This works well in areas such as the limbs. Otherwise, try applying finger pressure to the wound.

CHOKING

If a cat is fighting for air and gasping for breath, wrap it in a blanket or towel to immobilize it, and try to look in the mouth to see if there is any obstruction. While someone is calling the vet, you could try to dislocate the object by shining a small torch down the gullet and pulling the object out with a pair of tweezers. Take care you are not bitten. If a sharp object has been swallowed the problem should be dealt with by a vet. If the cat swallows a length of string or thread, do not pull it out. Leave it or tie the exposed end to an improvised collar so that it is not lost on the way to the vet.

FOREIGN BODIES

If grit, seeds or other objects become lodged in a cat's eyes or ears, you may be able to use ear or eye drops or olive oil to float them out. Do not use

tweezers in these areas. A cotton bud (swab) can sometimes be used gently to remove foreign bodies in the eye.

If potentially dangerous substances such as oil, paint or chemicals are spilt on a cat's coat, wash them off immediately with a dilute solution of mild detergent or soap and water. Patches of fur that are badly soiled should be cut off carefully and the area washed with soap and water.

◆ ABOVE
A cat that roams freely may have a more active and varied life, but it also runs a greater risk of accident and injury than the indoor pet.

◆ BELOW
Although cats can swim – and Turkish Van cats like this one are supposed to have a particular love of water – they will drown if enough water enters the lungs.

RESUSCITATION SITUATIONS

A completely collapsed cat which may appear dead can sometimes be resuscitated if you act swiftly. The condition most frequently occurs with a newly born kitten. It is very simple to assess if there is still a heartbeat by feeling for a pulse in the armpit. If no pulse is found it does not necessarily mean that brain death has occurred and you may still be able to resuscitate the animal by gently massaging the chest between finger and thumb and holding the head down.

HEART ATTACK

There has been a recent increase in the number of cats, especially pedigreed cats, who collapse and die of a condition called cardiomyopathy, of which there are various types. An apparently healthy cat may suddenly keel over and die. This condition is thought to run in families, but the mode of inheritance is unclear and is the subject of much research worldwide. Sometimes, in mild cases, massaging the chest between finger and thumb does help.

ELECTRIC SHOCK

A cat can sustain an electric shock as a result of chewing through electrical flexes and cords. Switch off the electricity immediately to prevent further shock. The vet's advice should be sought as severe burns to the gums and lips can result.

DROWNING

It takes very little liquid to cause drowning. All that is required is enough for the lungs to be filled so that oxygen is unable to enter the bloodstream. Patting the cat's back

HOW TO RESUSCITATE A CAT

There is no point in being squeamish if the cat's life is to be saved. A feline kiss of life is difficult to administer and will require coming into intimate oral contact with either the cat's nostrils or mouth. The instinct to save life is very strong so, for most owners, this aspect of resuscitation will not pose a problem.

1 Clear the airways of any vomit or blood and check that the tongue is pulled forward. Hold the cat's head gently backwards and blow into the nostrils. If the nostrils are restricted in some way, pinch the cat's mouth open with your fingers pressing both cheeks to create a restricted opening, take a deep breath and blow into the mouth. Do not overdo it, as a cat's lungs are very much smaller than a person's.

2 Between each breath, gently massage the chest to allow the air to trickle out, and maintain a rubbing motion on the cat's chest to try to stimulate heartbeat. Keep on with the mouth-to-mouth process until the cat can breath regularly by itself. It may be that this form of resuscitation does not work, in which case heart massage is the last option.

3 Heart massage may damage the cat. A delicate rubbing motion will just not stimulate the heart into beating so, with the cat on its side, preferably supported on a blanket or towel, press downwards firmly on the chest just behind the front leg, about once a second. In some cases, ribs have been broken in elderly animals, but the cat has survived. If this does not work, at least you know that you have done everything possible.

may be all that is needed to expel the water from the lungs, but more often drastic measures have to be employed such as swinging the cat by the hind legs in an attempt to get the liquid out. Then resuscitation can begin (*see box*).

ANIMAL BITES

The cat that roams freely outside is much more likely to come into contact with other animals than the house-bound feline. Fights over

territorial rights around the home are likely. The bite of any animal, including other cats, dogs, rodents and snakes, can be dangerous, as many bacteria are carried in the mouth.

It may not be immediately obvious that your cat has been bitten. Usually a cat that has been hurt will find a quiet, secluded spot to lick its wounds, quite literally. This is the cat's own first aid, as its saliva contains a natural antiseptic. You may not discover a

✦ LEFT
An Elizabethan (medical) collar is attached around the neck to prevent a cat from reaching back or down to lick a wound or medical dressing. The cat's owner then has to take on all grooming responsibilities.

IMMOBILIZING A CAT THAT IS FRIGHTENED OR IN PAIN

1 Place the towel on a table and the cat on the towel. Place one hand firmly on the cat's neck to control its head. Press the other firmly on the cat's back so that it lies down.

2 Keep one hand firmly on the cat's neck so that the head is under control throughout. With the other hand, bring the towel over the cat's neck, legs and body so that the legs are restrained.

3 Still keeping a firm but gentle hold on the neck, tuck the towel underneath the cat's body. Do not forget to talk to your pet in a calm voice all the time you are doing this.

hidden bite until you actually touch the site of the wound and the cat reacts. Keep the cat warm and comfortable and seek advice. Delay could mean that the cat will develop infection which will make treatment more complicated and therefore more traumatic for the cat. Wounds will need regular cleaning and bathing with a suitable antiseptic.

ABSCESSES

Any untreated puncture wound is liable to become infected and result in an abscess, which is a large, pus-filled swelling. Without treatment, the abscess may eventually burst, with a real risk of septicaemia (blood poisoning) due to toxins from the untreated abscess entering the bloodstream. The original puncture wounds soon heal, so the correct treatment will involve a trip to the vet so that the abscess can be lanced, allowing it to drain properly.

Septicaemia is serious, as it is with people. The onset is rapid and within hours a cat can be running a very high temperature. This may be followed by fits, sickness, a rapid fall of temperature to sub-normal level, collapse and death.

The greatest cause of an abscess is a bite or claw puncture from another cat. Such wounds are invariably sustained during a fight, so the most common abscess sites are around the head and neck, paws, and at the base of the tail.

SNAKE BITES

Many snake bites can be poisonous and may be followed by swelling around the wound, progressive lethargy and hyperventilation which may be accompanied by fits, followed by collapse and coma.

Once the wound site has been identified, try to apply a tourniquet above the punctures as quickly as possible (*see box*). The most likely site of a bite is on the leg, near the paws, in which case the tourniquet should be applied to the upper leg. If the wound is around the face or neck, then there is little that can be done.

When applying a tourniquet to a snake bite, the aim is to prevent the venom entering the bloodstream. However, remember that the application of a tourniquet cuts off the blood supply to the limb. The tourniquet should therefore be slackened every two to three minutes to ensure that the tissues are kept alive, even if this results in releasing a limited amount of the venom into the bloodstream. If this is not done, there is a possibility of such severe tissue damage that the limb would have to be amputated.

TO APPLY A TOURNIQUET

1 Place a loop of soft, narrow fabric, such as a stocking or a tie, around the limb, on the heart side of the wound site

2 Insert a pen, pencil, piece of cutlery or thin, strong stick between the skin and the fabric loop

3 Twist the fabric until it is tight enough to cut off the blood supply below it

4 Loosen the tourniquet for a few moments every two or three minutes and then re-tighten

5 If there is any swelling, apply a cold compress by wrapping a few ice cubes in a cloth, or (an athlete's tip) use a packet of frozen peas

6 Gently wash the affected spot with a recommended antiseptic, diluted to the manufacturer's instruction

7 Any bleeding should stop. If it does not, the tourniquet is not tight enough

8 Try to bandage the wound and take the cat to the vet as soon as possible. The wound may need stitching

◆ BELOW
If your cat is limping, the first action to take is to examine the paw for any foreign body, such as glass or a thorn, which may be lodged there.

◆ LEFT
A vet feels a cat's leg for any breakages in the bone or internal swellings that might suggest a sprain or arthritis, to find the cause of a limp.

STINGS

It is the cat's nature to chase and pounce on insects regardless of any danger. A single wasp sting is not too alarming but remember the wasp is able to sting repeatedly. Although a cat moves fast, a wasp tangled in the cat's fur can sting a number of times before it can be brushed off. In contrast, the bee leaves the sting behind in the cat. The bee sacrifices itself when it stings, and the full quota of bee venom is left behind. Stings can occur in the mouth or throat if the insect is swallowed. This will cause swelling, and breathing and swallowing might be restricted. If external this is unpleasant and painful; internally, it can be dangerous.

The cat may show an alarming allergic reaction to a sting. If the swelling has been caused by a bee sting, the actual sting remnant may be visible. This must be removed if possible, with tweezers. Whether the sting is internal or external, the cat should have veterinary attention without delay.

As a first-aid measure, external stings by bees or wasps may be treated with a commercially available antihistamine cream or lotion. If this is not immediately available, simple home remedies can be used. Bee stings can be treated with alkaline substances such as bicarbonate of soda, whereas wasp stings respond to the application of an acid such as vinegar. The cat should not be allowed to lick at any of these substances.

POISONING

Cats are great wanderers and they may well walk through any range of toxic materials. Transferred to the mouth through washing, such substances can easily cause poisoning, and burning to contact areas. Thorough washing of paws with a mild shampoo followed by thorough rinsing will alleviate some of the pain before the vet is involved. Vomiting, lassitude, apparent blindness, convulsions and collapse are all signs of poisoning. If such symptoms occur, seek veterinary aid immediately.

It is inadvisable to try to find a way of easing the animal's suffering yourself beyond keeping the cat warm and quiet. Take a sample of the substance if you know what it is, or note the name, so that an antidote may be found quickly if available. Your vet will have access to the national poison hotline. In some countries, where stray animals are a

◆ ABOVE
Give a cat a toy to play with in the garden, and with a bit of luck, this may distract it from pursuing the local wildlife.

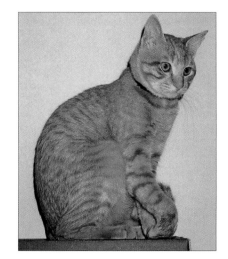

◆ ABOVE
A vital nerve was severed in this cat's foreleg. The cause was barely visible – a tiny puncture in the skin, perhaps from a barbed wire fence or an animal bite. There was no improvement after a month, and the leg was amputated, but the cat continued to lead an active outdoor life.

BANDAGING A LEG

1 One person should hold the cat, and the other apply the dressing. Place lint over the injured area and hold it in place with your hand.

2 Use the bandage to bind the lint into position by taking it down over the paw and back up again; then wind it around the leg.

3 Continue winding the bandage firmly (but not so tight that the blood supply is cut off) and evenly around the entire length of the leg.

4 Split the end of the bandage leaving two ends long enough to take back around the leg in opposite directions. Tie the two ends together.

5 Tape adhesive bandage over the end of the paw and back up again as before. Wind around the entire length of the leg.

6 Keep the cat indoors for as long as the dressing is on. Change the dressing regularly as advised by the vet, or when it becomes grubby or loose.

nuisance, cats and dogs are sometimes deliberately poisoned by those who consider them pests.

If your cat returns home covered in motor oil, it is important to remove the oil from the coat immediately, as it could poison the cat's digestive system and result in kidney damage. Use a mild household detergent in lots of warm water, and seek veterinary advice if in difficulty.

SCRAPES AND BRUISES

Bruises are much less easy to detect than cuts, though you will suspect their presence if the cat becomes unusually unhappy about your touching the spot where the bruise is rooted. Similar signs are apparent if an abscess is developing on the site. As with human bruises, some come to the surface of the skin reasonably rapidly, whereas deep-seated bruising can take days to work its way out. Seek professional advice if

in doubt. Bruises and contusions respond very well to the application of *Hamamelis virginiana* (witch-hazel). Although such a remedy can be taken orally in very limited doses, it is better to prevent the cat from licking off any application by putting a medical collar around the neck.

STRAINS AND LIMPS

The cat may limp and resort to excessive washing of the injured spot. If you suspect something is amiss, first examine the paw carefully to see if there is a splinter or thorn in it, and remove it with tweezers if possible. Disinfect the area and keep your eye on the cat. Confine the cat indoors, and if there is no improvement, ask the vet to have a look at it.

If the problem is a strain, a cat will not rest of its own accord, and continued physical activity could not only aggravate the strain but also prevent it from healing.

BURNS

Cats attracted by cooking smells may leap on to unguarded cooking areas and even into ovens, and may be scalded by spilled hot liquid. A cat may also receive appalling burns, externally and internally, if it comes into contact with any of the lethal chemicals to be found in the house and garden.

Once the skin is burned, the body institutes its own first-aid regime. Body fluids are rushed to the affected area, and a blister forms protecting the underlying tissue. Do not burst the blister as the fluid in it helps to prevent infection. You can bathe the burn with ice-cold water until all heat has been taken out of the damaged area. Call the vet.

You can also apply a sterile, dry dressing loosely over the burn to keep out infection. Do not apply greasy substances – this would be like putting butter into a hot frying pan.

STANDARD TREATMENTS

✦ BELOW LEFT
A two-week-old kitten is still gaining some immunity from infection through its mother's milk – as long as the mother herself has been kept fully up-to-date with her inoculations.

However hardy your cat is, it runs the risk of being struck down by a killer virus infection unless it is inoculated and boosted on a regular basis. If a cat contracts one of the diseases for which preventative vaccines are available, it is very serious, for there is no treatment that can be guaranteed to save it. All a vet can do is to treat the symptoms and minimize suffering, and hope that your pet's natural immunity will fight the illness.

INOCULATIONS

In the first few days of its life, a kitten's resistance is boosted by the antibody-rich colostrum that is the mother's first milk. Although this is replaced by normal milk after the first few days, this also contains some antibodies so, as long as the kittens are feeding, the mother's immunity will pass down to them through the milk. As soon as weaning starts, this natural protection diminishes. From now on, immunity has to be built up actively by the kitten and will no longer be acquired passively from the queen. Active immunity can be built up by exposure to infections or, more safely and securely, by inoculations. Taking your cat to the vet to be inoculated is a vital part of routine care. Inoculations are given at 9–12 weeks; the kitten is then kept in for a week or two to prevent exposure to infection while the aquired immunity from the vaccine becomes effective. Inoculations subsequently need to be boosted every year. Some kittens or adult cats may feel a little under par for a few days after first inoculations or the annual booster, but it is rare for there to be any major problems.

FREEDOM FROM WORRY

Over the past 30 years, there have been enormous steps forward in the prevention and cure of feline ailments. The diseases that used to pose the greatest risk to pedigreed and non-pedigreed felines alike, are no longer a problem if the regular, recommended inoculation programme is followed.

✦ LEFT
Six-week-old kittens may be introduced to new social experiences, but three weeks before their first vaccination, they must not be exposed to other cats in the outside world.

◆ BELOW
A stray cat with its single-kitten litter. The mother's tough and probably deprived lifestyle may have limited her ability to produce a bigger litter.

◆ BELOW
A kitten receives its first vaccination at six to nine weeks of age. It will have to be kept indoors for another two to three weeks after it has received its second vaccination.

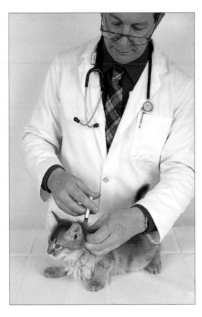

WHICH INOCULATIONS?

Recommendations regarding vaccinations vary in different countries. In the United States, for instance, where, in urban areas, owners are often advised to keep their cats indoors, both cat flu viruses, feline infectious enteritis (feline distemper) and rabies are considered the core inoculations. Those against chlamydia,

feline leukaemia virus and feline infectious peritonitis are often considered necessary only for cats likely to be exposed to risk in the outside world. However, bear in mind that your cat could escape and come into contact with one of the diseases you decided not to inoculate against. Take your vet's advice.

THE KILLERS

The most serious infections are: cat flu (viral rhinitis), which encompasses two viruses that affect the cat's upper respiratory tract; feline infectious enteritis; chlamydia; and feline leukaemia virus. Rabies should be added to the list in countries where the disease is known to exist. Although these are not the only viruses to affect the cat, these are the major viral conditions that have wrought havoc in the past among domestic cats.

Effective vaccines against cat flu and feline enteritis have been around for several years. A vaccine to treat the leukaemia virus is a more recent

addition. As yet, in the United Kingdom, where rabies does not exist, the vaccine can only be administered by authorised vets to cats that are going to countries where the disease exists.

GENERAL CHECK-UP

The vet will only inoculate your cat if it is in good health, so do not take it if it is below par for any reason. At the same time as the annual booster vaccinations, ask the vet to give your cat a check-up – to look at ears, teeth, gums and general condition. With luck, this will be the only time the vet sees your cat. You can also stock up with treatments for worms and fleas.

◆ BELOW
A Chocolate Silver Ocicat kitten at 15 weeks old has had all its vaccinations, and is independent of its mother.

WHAT TO DO WHEN

◆ 9 weeks: first vaccination

◆ 12 weeks: second vaccination

◆ 16 weeks: spaying for females

◆ 4–6 months: neutering (altering) for males

◆ 6 months: start flea treatment

◆ monthly (after 6 months): renew flea treatment

◆ every 6 months: worm treatment

◆ every year: booster vaccinations and check-up

◆ BELOW
A recently spayed female shows the shaved area
where the incision was made. There is a slight
possibility that the fur may grow back a
different colour in this area.

NEUTERING (ALTERING)

Neutering, altering or desexing not only prevents reproduction but also the inconvenience of the female cat coming into heat (oestrus) or calling. In the female cat this is called spaying. In the male the operation, castration, reduces the tendency to spray and also the odour of the male cat's urine.

The operation has the effect of modifying behaviour associated with sexual desire and establishing and marking territory (see the chapter on *Behaviour and Intelligence*). The result is that the desexed cat is usually more stable and affectionate, and bonds more easily with the family. Recent work in Britain and the United States has shown that the operation in either sex can be carried out earlier than was

◆ BELOW
Burmillas are generally known for their good nature, but any aggressive tendencies will be further modified by the desexing process.

previously thought with no ill effects. Some rescue organizations now desex kittens before they are homed at eight to twelve weeks, but the majority of vets prefer to carry out the operation when the kitten is older, at four to six months. As both operations are carried out under a general anaesthetic, no food or water can be taken for about 12 hours beforehand. The operation cannot be reversed in either sex.

CASTRATION

The operation involves the removal, under general anaesthetic, of the cat's testes. Tiny incisions are involved and usually no stitches are necessary. Within 24 hours the cat is usually back to normal. Both kittens and adult cats can be castrated. If you consider giving a home to a stray tom, castration will ensure that he settles quickly, is less aggressive, less territorial and less

likely to roam. This also means that he is less likely to pick up infections and be involved in traffic accidents.

SPAYING

Female cats do not miss motherhood, and gain security, as they no longer have the urge to roam when coming into heat or calling, and are no longer targeted by unneutered (unaltered) male cats. Spaying or altering the female cat is more complicated than in the male. The cat's ovaries (where the eggs are produced) and womb (uterus) are removed to prevent her coming into heat. She should not be on heat at the time of the operation. A small area of fur is shaved on the abdomen and an incision made, which has to be stitched afterwards. The spayed female cat is usually back to normal quickly but will appreciate care, warmth and light meals for about a week, until the stitches are taken out.

How Long will your Cat Live?

♦ BELOW
A Blue Bi-colour Persian father seems to contemplate the continuation of his pedigreed line with one of his kittens.

From about the age of ten to twelve years, a cat may begin to show signs of growing old. This may not be immediately apparent as the slowing down process is very gradual. Internal organs may not work as well as they once did and joints may become that little bit stiffer. Over time the cat seems to restrict its activities, is far less playful and becomes a creature of sedentary habits. Particular health conditions such as diabetes or arthritis require constant supervision and medical intervention.

The oldest cat recorded was a tabby called Puss who was said to have lived for 36 years. The oldest pedigreed cat on record is Sukoo, a Siamese who died in 1989, at the age of 31 years. These are exceptional ages, however. Most cats live for about 14–16 years and a few may reach 20 years. With pedigreed cats there is a very accurate means of determining age, as they are normally registered with an exact date of birth and registration number.

When you first get a 12-week-old kitten, it is very likely that its lifespan will be something between ten and fifteen years. This could mean that the cat will become a companion to your children as well as to yourself. A longer life is not unusual, in which case it may well live to see your grandchildren as well. To borrow from the dog world, a cat is for life, not just for Christmas. This has to be thoroughly understood before a kitten joins the household.

Neutered (altered) cats have a slightly longer lifespan than those which remain unneutered. This is particularly true of male cats. An unneutered (unaltered) tom will fight to defend territory and the resulting injuries and infections may shorten his life. Females lead a much quieter life, and a career spent having kittens, in an environment in which her condition is well-maintained, appears to have little effect on the female's longevity.

Apart from differing nutritional requirements at various stages of its life, a cat's physical responses slow down as it gets older and joints become stiff. This not only has the effect of reducing suppleness and agility, but has implications for the daily care of the cat such as grooming.

♦ RIGHT
The start of a long relationship: this kitten will probably live long enough to be a companion for its young owner throughout her childhood and teenage years.

COPING WITH DEATH

When the end comes, it can be rapid, as though a clockwork motor has run down. Very old cats settle into a routine which reflects their capabilities. It seems important for a cat to maintain its dignity to a degree greater, even, than that of many other animals. This can be extremely difficult when the efficacy of bodily functions is being challenged by old age. A few elderly cats are distressed by the loss of vital sensory equipment through deafness or blindness. Grooming becomes difficult as flexibility is reduced, and incontinence may occur, both of which can upset the naturally fastidious cat.

Your cat may die in its sleep but this does not happen often. If, however, it is suffering from ailments that give it chronic pain or prevent it from responding to its natural instincts, you need seriously to consider how kind it is to keep it alive. A vet can end an animal's life painlessly on the request of its owner. The cat is injected with an overdose of anaesthetic which literally puts it to sleep. Many vets will allow you to be present for your pet's last moments, if you wish. Others can only advise; the

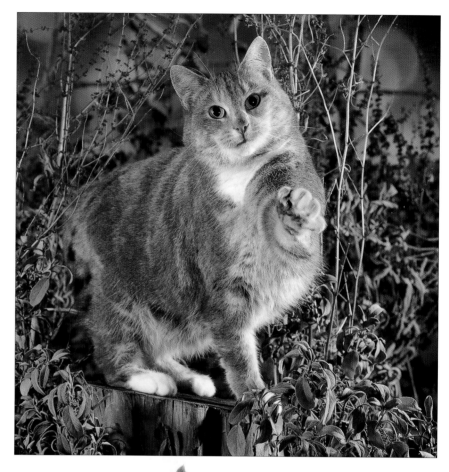

✦ ABOVE
A rather portly middle-aged cat that will have to lose some weight if it is to have a healthy and trouble-free old age.

✦ BELOW
Producing two to three litters a year has left this 10-year-old farm cat with a sagging stomach. It would be kind to have her spayed.

✦ ABOVE
A 10-year-old tabby and white that could well have several more years of contented living as long as a healthy diet is maintained and disease and infection do not strike.

owner must make the decision, except in exceptional circumstances when the vet takes responsibility. Euthanasia can be regarded as a final gift to an animal that has shared your life.

MOURNING

The natural lifespan of a cat is a fraction of human life expectancy, and yet a cat may be a day-to-day companion over a significant section of your life, such as your entire childhood.
When your cat dies, you may consider burying it in the garden, in a favoured snoozing spot, for instance. If not, there are pet cemeteries where cremation or burial can be carried out.

There will inevitably be a period of mourning which may, initially at least, feel as intense as it would for a member of your human family. This is quite normal. You have lost a member of the family and a very special one. This is

◆ RIGHT
Two old friends have aged in different ways. Perhaps the overweight male on the chair should give up his seat for the thin and frail female.

the little furry body that snuggled up to you when you were feeling ill, depressed or annoyed. You will remember the rumbling purr of greeting and trust, and the times when you could not express your feelings to anyone else but the little cat that listened and soothed you into eventually finding a solution.

◆ LEFT
An 8-week-old Cream Burmese kitten with a lifetime ahead of it, lives for the moment with its toys.

◆ ABOVE RIGHT
A cat grows old with dignity and favours warm spots such as the top of the stove, but beware of the danger a hot stove may present.

◆ RIGHT
A gravestone and rose commemorate the passing of a much-loved cat.

INDEX